Also by David Lehman

POETRY

New and Selected Poems (2013)
Yeshiva Boys (2009)
When a Woman Loves a Man (2005)
The Evening Sun (2002)
The Daily Mirror (2000)
Valentine Place (1996)
Operation Memory (1990)
An Alternative to Speech (1986)

COLLABORATIONS

Poetry Forum (with Judith Hall) (2007)
Jim and Dave Defeat the Masked Man (with James Cummins; drawings by Archie Rand) (2005)

NONFICTION

Sinatra's Century: One Hundred Notes on the Man and His World (2015)
The State of the Art: A Chronicle of American Poetry, 1988–2014 (2015)
A Fine Romance: Jewish Songwriters, American Songs (2009)
The Last Avant-Garde: The Making of the New York School of Poets (1998)
The Big Question (1995)
The Line Forms Here (1992)
Signs of the Times: Deconstruction and the Fall of Paul de Man (1991)
The Perfect Murder: A Study in Detection (1989)

EDITED BY DAVID LEHMAN

The Best American Poetry (series editor)
The Best American Erotic Poems: From 1800 to the Present (2008)
The Oxford Book of American Poetry (2006)
Great American Prose Poems: From Poe to the Present (2003)
The KGB Bar Book of Poems (with Star Black) (2000)
Ecstatic Occasions, Expedient Forms (1996)
James Merrill: Essays in Criticism (with Charles Berger) (1983)
Beyond Amazement: New Essays on John Ashbery (1980)

Poems in the Manner Of

David Lehman

SCRIBNER POETRY

New York   London   Toronto   Sydney   New Delhi

Scribner Poetry
An Imprint of Simon & Schuster, Inc.
1230 Avenue of the Americas
New York, NY 10020

First Scribner trade paperback edition March 2017

SCRIBNER POETRY and design are registered trademarks of The Gale Group, Inc., used under license by Simon & Schuster, Inc., the publisher of this work.

For information about special discounts for bulk purchases, please contact Simon & Schuster Special Sales at 1-866-506-1949 or business@simonandschuster.com.

The Simon & Schuster Speakers Bureau can bring authors to your live event. For more information or to book an event, contact the Simon & Schuster Speakers Bureau at 1-866-248-3049 or visit our website at www.simonspeakers.com.

Interior design by Erich Hobbing

Manufactured in the United States of America

10   9   8   7   6   5   4   3   2   1

Library of Congress Cataloging-in-Publication Data
Names: Lehman, David, [date] author.
Title: Poems in the manner of / David Lehman.
Description: First Scribner trade paperback edition. | New York : Scribner Poetry, 2017.
Identifiers: LCCN 2016024905 | ISBN 9781501137396 (softcover : acid-free paper) | ISBN 9781501137419 (ebook)
Subjects: | BISAC: POETRY / American / General. | POETRY / General.
Classification: LCC PS3562.E428 A6 2017 | DDC 811/.54—dc23
LC record available at https://lccn.loc.gov/2016024905

ISBN 978-1-5011-3739-6
ISBN 978-1-5011-3741-9 (ebook)

Contents

Introduction   xiii

Part One

Two Poems in the Manner of Catullus (To a Critic;
    To a Rival)—(84 BCE–54 BCE)   3
Poem in the Manner of Li Po—(701–762)   5
Poem in the Manner of Lady Murasaki—(c. 978–c. 1014–1025)   6
Poem in the Manner of Iago [i.e., Shakespeare]—
    (1564–April 23, 1616)   9
Poem in the Manner of Polonius [i.e., Shakespeare]—
    (1564–April 23, 1616)   11
Hamlet, Interpreted [i.e., Shakespeare]—(1564–April 23, 1616)   12
Two Poems in the Courtly Manner—[17th century poetry]   16
Poem in the Manner of Bashō—(1644–1694)   18
For I Will Consider Your Dog Molly [after Christopher Smart]—
    (April 11, 1722–May 21, 1771)   19
Goethe's Nightsong [after Johann Wolfgang von Goethe:
    a translation]—(August 28, 1749–March 22, 1832)   22

Part Two

Autumn Evening [after Friedrich Hölderlin]—
    (March 20, 1770–June 7, 1843)   25
Cento: The True Romantics   26
Poem in the Manner of William Wordsworth—
    (April 7, 1770–April 23 1850)   27

On This Day I Do Not Enter My Sixth-and-Thirtieth Year
    [Lord Byron]—(January 22, 1788–April 19, 1824)   29

Poem in the Manner of John Keats—(October 31, 1795–
    February 23, 1821)   30

On Keats's Birthday—(October 31, 1795–February 23, 1821)   31

Poem in the Manner of Walt Whitman—(May 31, 1819–
    March 26, 1892)   34

Poem in the Manner of Charles Baudelaire—(April 9, 1821–
    August 31, 1867)   36

Let's Beat Up Some Beggars! [after Baudelaire: a translation]—
    (April 9, 1821–August 31, 1867)   37

Poem in the Manner of Emily Dickinson—
    (December 10, 1830–May 15, 1886)   39

The Hapless Hour [after Thomas Hardy]—[June 2, 1840–
    January 11, 1928]   40

Poem in the Manner of Gerard Manley Hopkins—
    (July 28, 1844–June 8, 1889)   41

Poem in the Manner of Arthur Rimbaud—(October 20, 1854–
    November 10, 1891)   42

Part Three

Freud Quiz [Sigmund Freud]—(May 6, 1856–
    September 23, 1939)   45

Poem in the Manner of C. P. Cavafy—(April 29, 1863–
    April 29, 1933)   56

Poem in the Manner of William Butler Yeats—(June 13, 1865–
    January 28, 1939)   57

Poem in the Manner of Gertrude Stein—(February 3, 1874–
    July 27, 1946)   58

Poem in the Manner of Robert Frost—(March 26, 1874–
    January 29, 1963)   59

Poem in the Manner of Rainer Maria Rilke—
    (December 4, 1875–December 29, 1926)   60

Poem in the Manner of Max Jacob [loose translation]—
(July 12, 1876–March 5, 1944)   61

Poem in the Manner of Wallace Stevens (October 2, 1879–
August 2, 1955)   63

The Matador of Metaphor [after Wallace Stevens]—
(October 2, 1879–August 2, 1955)   64

Poem in the Manner of Wallace Stevens as Rewritten
by Gertrude Stein   65

Zone [after Guillaume Apollinaire: a translation]—
(August 25, 1880–November 9, 1918)   66

Hotel [after Apollinaire: a translation]—(August 25, 1880–
November 9, 1918)   72

Poem in the Manner of Virginia Woolf—(January 25, 1882–
March 28, 1941)   73

On Kafka's Birthday [Franz Kafka]—(July 3, 1883–
June 3, 1924)   75

Poem in the Manner of William Carlos Williams—
(September 17, 1883–March 4, 1963)   77

Poem in the Manner of Ezra Pound—(October 30, 1885–
November 1, 1972)   79

Two Poems in the Manner of Edna St. Vincent Millay—
(February 22, 1892–October 19, 1950)   81

Brooklyn Bridge [after Mayakovsky: a translation]—
(July 19, 1893–April 14, 1930)   83

Poem in the Manner of Vladimir Mayakovsky—
(July 19, 1893–April 14, 1930)   90

Poem in the Manner of Dorothy Parker—(August 22, 1893–
June 7, 1967)   91

Poem in the Manner of Marianne Moore—
(November 15, 1897–February 5, 1972)   92

Poem Ending in a Phrase by Federico García Lorca—
(June 5, 1898–August 19, 1936)   93

Poem in the Manner of Henri Michaux—(May 24, 1899–
October 19, 1984)   95

Poem in the Manner of Ernest Hemingway—(July 21, 1899–
July 2, 1961)   96
Poem in the Manner of Jorge Luis Borges—(August 24, 1899–
June 14, 1986)   97

Part Four

Poem in the Manner of Pablo Neruda—(July 12, 1904–
September 23, 1973)   101
Poem in the Manner of W. H. Auden—(February 21, 1907–
September 29, 1973)   102
Due Diligence (after W. H. Auden)—(February 21, 1907–
September 29, 1973)   103
Poem in the Manner of an Eric Ambler Spy Novel—
(June 28, 1909–October 22, 1998)   105
Poem in the Manner of Robert Lowell—(March 1, 1917–
September 12, 1977)   107
Poem Based on a Line from Gwendolyn Brooks—
(June 7, 1917–December 3, 2000)   109
Poem in the Manner of Charles Bukowski—(August 16, 1920–
March 9, 1994)   110
Ode on Punctuation [after Kenneth Koch]—
(February 27, 1925–July 6, 2002)   111
On Marilyn Monroe's Birthday [after Frank O'Hara]—
(March 27, 1926–July 25, 1966)   113
08/22/08 [after Frank O'Hara]—(March 27, 1926–
July 25, 1966)   115
Poem in the Manner of Sylvia Plath—[October 27, 1932–
February 11, 1963]   117
Poem in the Manner of Susan Sontag—(January 16, 1933–
December 28, 2004)   118
I Remember [after Joe Brainard]—(March 11, 1941–
May 25, 1994)   120

Part Five

Poem in the Prophetic Manner   127

Prose Poem in the Classic French Manner   129

Poem in the Manner of the 1940s   130

Poem in the Manner of the 1950s   132

Poem in the Manner of the 1960s   134

On the Lives of the Modern Poets   135

Poem Inspired by the Mind of T. S. Eliot   137

Cento: In a Drear-Nighted December   138

Highway 61 (Revisited)   139

Poem in the Manner of a Jazz Standard   141

Poem in the Manner of a Hit Song by Harold Arlen and
    Johnny Mercer, c. 1945   142

Acknowledgments   143

Introduction

In April 2002, I began writing "poems in the manner of" some of my favorite poets—the ones who had made a deep impression on me when I started writing poetry in college and the years immediately after. The idea took hold. By the end of May I had written drafts of poems provoked by Baudelaire, Rimbaud, Rilke, Hölderlin, Marianne Moore, Apollinaire, Mayakovsky, Auden, Gertrude Stein, and Henri Michaux. The pace slowed down considerably, but the idea never went away, and incrementally this book began to take shape.

Among the poems that triggered the project were two by Ted Berrigan in *The Sonnets*: "Poem in the Traditional Manner" and "Poem in the Modern Manner." I had in mind the shibboleth that in the writing of poetry, to have a distinctive "voice" is everything. There is a counterview, demonstrated by Fernando Pessoa, inventor of "heteronyms," that the poet should adopt as many names, personae, masks—call them what you will—as suits his or her personality.[1] The larger idea is that style is misunderstood; it is not the end in itself but the means to an indefinable end that, as Wallace Stevens wrote in "Man Carrying Thing" (1947), "must resist the intelligence / Almost successfully."

From the start I wanted "in the manner of" to be a flexible category embracing homage, parody, imitation, and appropriation, or combinations of these four things. Some of the poems in this book borrow lines or an organizing conceit from the poet named in the title. "Poem in the Manner of Bashō," "Goethe's Nightsong," "Let's Beat Up Some Beggars!," "Zone," "Hotel," and "Brooklyn Bridge" are translations of poems by Bashō, Goethe, Baudelaire, Apollinaire, Apollinaire, and Mayakovsky, respectively. Inspired by a high-spirited effort by Larry Fagin, "Poem in the Manner of Max Jacob" retains the structure of the French original but Americanizes the content. Two poems exemplify

1. I drew sustenance, too, from Valéry Larbaud's nom de plume, Ezra Pound's "personae," and William Butler Yeats's masks.

varieties of the cento, a poem consisting exclusively of lines culled from earlier works.

As more poems were written, and a file became a manuscript in progress, I broadened the idea, writing poems "in the manner of" a period, a style, a mood. Not every effort worked out. I have written and shelved many more "poems in the manner of" than are included here. No matter how much time I devoted to them, I never completed to my satisfaction the poems I had set out to write in the manner of Blake and Coleridge, Emerson and Hart Crane, a Bessie Smith blues and an example of Japanese linked verse (renga). But my aim was not to be comprehensive in the manner of a certain type of anthology or critical survey but to honor my own influences and impulses in the hope that the end product warrants the reader's attention. I wanted to make the case for the value of imitation as a creative strategy—and for the related idea that a formal decision may precede or even dictate content.

In addressing my influences, I veered from the strictly literary and turned to Freud among others. I have not resisted using ad hoc forms— the multiple-choice test, the piece of prose on the fence between a short story and an essay, the astrological profile—any more than I could resist writing a poem in the manner of a jazz standard. In the pieces on Hamlet and John Keats, the astrological terms are laid on pretty thick but tongue in cheek. The pieces proceed on the nervy assumption that the horoscope may resemble one or another of the "usual pastimes" that T. S. Eliot lists in "The Dry Salvages": "haruspicate or scry," "sortilege, or tea leaves," playing cards, pentagrams, handwriting analysis, palm reading, and the "pre-conscious terrors" of the dreaming mind. As Eliot's use of the tarot deck in *The Waste Land* proves, such pastimes may be a bust at prediction but may serve as the means of poetic exploration.

I hope I have produced a unified book of poems that conveys a thesis about the pleasures of poetic influence. If I have done my job, aspiring poets will look at this book and attempt their own poems "in the manner of" the poets they most admire. With this possibility in mind, and to provide an autobiographical context, I wrote the brief head notes preceding the poems.

The order of the poems is chronological by the date of birth of the poem's designated precursor. Poems "in the manner of" something other than an individual writer were filed where intuition led.

Part One

The unexpurgated Catullus is the most bawdy and profane of poets. He hurls insults with brutal candor and makes the reader feel like doing the same.

Two Poems in the Manner of Catullus

1. To a Critic

You made the mistake of praising my pain,
Flavius. This the connoisseurs of cool,
whose approval you seek and shall never gain,
could not condone. You should have known better.
They made you feel like a fool.
You joined in the laughter but it felt bitter.

And ever since you have panned
all work of my hand
with the result that I, too, despise you,
and I do not wish you well.
Yet I took no pleasure when I heard Junius tell
Calista your wife had cuckolded you

with her yoga teacher the same week
you faced a tax audit and ate a steak
with a side of fried poison, missed your train
and lost your job. I feel your pain,
Flavius. Not even a shmuck
like you deserves such lousy luck.

2. To a Rival

More beautiful than daffodils
in February or the face
that is always turned away
from the earth was Diana
a dance major at the High
School of Performing Arts
whose legs were long when
skirts were short, and what
was she doing with you
Junius, lecherous bastard who
tried to fuck every girl he met:
how could she fall for your shit?
Though I was born with a stutter,
Junius, I will denounce you yet
and win awards for my oratory
in a full session of parliament

When Ezra Pound translated Li Po, arguably the greatest poet in China's Tang dynasty, he revolutionized two things at once: the craft of translation and the tone of modern poetry. He set the precedent that allows poets to translate from languages they do not know.

Poem in the Manner of Li Po

In the Tai-T'ien mountains
the master has gone who knows where
I search for his absence

    With wine I, too, am absent
    from the night

Petals fall after the storm
down secret streams I see
the ghost of a yellow moon

    There are other heavens
    than are known to you and me

When I read Lady Murasaki's *Tale of Genji* in New York in 1973, what enchanted me most was the notion that you could punctuate a narrative with a haiku, a little like the way an aria punctuates an opera.

Poem in the Manner of Lady Murasaki

In the mist and gloom of twilight the prince, disguised in civilian clothes, approached Masuda Pond. Under a large gray rock glinting in the sunlight with brown, green, red, and blue layers of stone, he left a note for the young wife to decipher:

In the Eighth Month the nights grow long,
But the moon comes nearer than wind to the land.

Abandoned by her husband, who had traveled to the mainland on orders of his warlord, the Akashi lady blushed with an intensity of longing that surprised and frightened her. She thought:

I wonder who lives the fulfilled life:
The faithful wife or the ghost of her desire?

It was then that Genji remembered the shell of the locust: hollow, inanimate, yet it gave him the strength to confront a world of unrest. He gave the shell, attached to a long reed, to a boy who had earned his trust, and told him to bring it to the abandoned lady.

The wind carries my words to you,
Though you hear only the wind in the reeds.

And she of the white cheeks thought:

To be remembered is to be loved
If only until the frost nips the leaves.

Though the murmuring crowd expected him in Lotus Hall for
the forty-ninth-day lamentations, Genji contrived to return to Masuda
Pond. He dressed his lieutenant in his red satin robes and his ivory mask
for the procession of scrolls. Then he trained the younger man for the
ceremony, down to the minutest details. The apprentice imitated his
master as a translator imitates a noble author of renown. When the day
came, the congregants felt the spirit of Genji among them as they prayed
for a bounty of grace. Disguised as a peasant Genji himself crossed the
Uji River at daybreak and descended upon the bald scholar who had
tutored him in Chinese poetry. To his mentor he confided his misgivings:

The lady has a single tear on her cheek, her husband gone,
But shall the prince reveal his love and not his name?

Slowly the elderly scholar and his eternal student sipped their
Gyokuro tea. The prince said two words: "jade dew." Delighted, his old
professor ventured the opinion that the lady in question understood
that the man comforting her had a secret identity. But (he added) "she is
too well-bred to demand an explanation."

In the house of the "evening faces," the maidservants wondered
what had happened to the Akashi lady. Had the wanton son of Chúko
Province spirited her off to the "cloud of smoke"?

Genji suppressed a laugh. He wrote:

The lake is a cloud of smoke,
But there is no light in the mist of morn

On Masuda Pond, there followed three days of blissful serenity and no noise except the tunes of birds, the chirp of insects, the wind in the reeds, the belching frogs.

When Man and Woman speak without words
They hear the secret music of the world.

When the three days ended, the Akashi lady cried. Despite her protests, Genji returned her to her cabin and bade her swear to greet her husband with a feast upon his return from the wars.

The prince let no one see him weep. Disguising his handwriting he wrote on a fallen leaf:

Autumn will end, all things must end,
But when summer returns with her robes, shall I cease to cry?

Iago's cunning use of the phrase "put money in thy purse" (*Othello*, act 1, scene 3) inspired these variations in the spirit of that cruel rhetorician.

Poem in the Manner of Iago

Put money in thy purse,
Thy purpose make money.

As brokers sell short
and buy on the dips—

As waiters wait for tips—

As litigants in court
rake in the chips—

Make money thy end,
By all means make money.

*

Let poverty be a curse
for others to bear
with dust on their lips
and ash in their hair

Let the buyer beware

Put thy trust
in no friend
even if he swear
Do what you must
But make money.

*

You will die
and when you lie
beneath the ground
you will hear no sound

Go ahead, right some wrongs,
write speeches or fatuous folk songs

Reserve an expensive hearse

Put money in thy purse,
I say make money.

The most famous statement of advice from a father to a son is Polonius's speech to Laertes in *Hamlet* with its injunction "to thine oneself be true." From Polonius's "neither a borrower nor a lender be," I derived "neither a follower nor a leader be," and took off from there.

Poem in the Manner of Polonius

Neither a follower nor a leader be.
Vote, but tell no one for whom you voted.
Do not avoid jury duty. Avoid a fight,
but if attacked, fight back with all your might,

and don't try to get laid on your first date.
Kiss her good night and call the next day.
Memorize verse, laws, and amendments
to the Constitution. Obey the Ten Commandments.

Eat when hungry, have a drink when you need one,
and remember to have fun
at least once a week, and not to forget whose son
you are. Take your vitamins. Sign no one's petition.

Travel light, and don't forget a sweater
when you wander in the dark talking aloud
to a mother or a lover though no one's there.
Look up at the sky, and see God in a cloud.

The astrological profile as a form for a prose poem allows not only for humor but for permission to treat falsehoods and rumors as though they were facts.

Hamlet, Interpreted

—an astrological profile

Hamlet was born in Copenhagen, Denmark, on August 10, 1599, a Monday, at 8:11 AM. He wrote two novels and three books of poems, but it was as an actor and director that he gained great renown. He won two "best actor" Oscars, one for "best director," and a Grammy for his part in an ensemble performance of the best "best song" Oscars from 1936 until 1965. His career as a secret agent for the Americans in Vienna in the years immediately following World War II was disclosed only after his death. He played a pivotal part in an affair of intrigue centering on the itinerary of Dimitrios Makropoulos, the most notorious terrorist of the era, whose plot to sabotage the 1952 summer Olympics in Helsinki was foiled by a team of agents captained by Hamlet.[1]

A Leo with Sagittarius rising and Saturn opposing his sun, Hamlet taught himself English in Elsinore, quickly grew fluent in his adopted tongue, and wrote all of his books and plays in English after the initial book-length essay he wrote in Danish under Kierkegaard's influence, *Both / And: The Aesthetic Way*. His natal chart predicts a great career cut short. Except for his untimely death, Hamlet has the most enviable

---

1. Charles Latimer's crisp account in *The Intercom Conspiracy* is a salutary corrective to more breathless versions of this memorable affair.

destiny of any princely male: handsome, brilliant, athletic, creative. Though prone to melancholic periods, and excessively self-conscious, he was impulsive but without the overweening arrogance and wrath that make Achilleus a less sympathetic example of the type. In Hades, Achilleus told Odysseus that he would sooner be a laborer toiling for a poor farmer on earth than king of all the dead, a remark that Hamlet would not have made without adding an ironic paradox. Rhetorical flourishes came to him spur of the moment: "O God, I could be bounded in a nutshell and count myself a king of infinite space, were it not that I have bad dreams": a pair of hyperboles terminating in an understatement consisting of eight quick monosyllables.[2]

Hamlet's Venus in Gemini suggests a marked ambivalence in his love life. He looked tough in a leather jacket and smoked as brilliantly as Bette Davis or the underrated Fred MacMurray. His moon in Taurus signifies a philosophical cast of mind and the tendency to go it alone rather than travel with an entourage. His Mercury in Aquarius conjunct with the lightning bolt of Uranus makes it no surprise to learn that he is swift of foot and quick of mind. The emphatic placement of his Mars is in Leo, for he is on a mission even if he knows not what it is. His Jupiter in Sagittarius indicates great intellectual curiosity, encyclopedic in range, despite saturnine bouts of depression.

At Harvard, Hamlet studied art and literature, joined the fencing team (foil), and wrote dance criticism for *The Advocate*. His success at fencing (first place in the Ivy League finals) he attributed to "continual practice."[3] He also played chess and tennis. A Rhodes Scholarship took him to Oxford (Balliol College) and he spent his "long vacs" in Paris,

---

2. Hamlet's rejoinders are legendary. When asked whether he considered himself a decisive person, he said "yes and no" but with an ironic grin that made everyone present feel they were in on the joke. In his diary, he devotes a short essay to the shades of difference between and among "procrastination," "hesitation," "irresolution," and "deliberation." He also contrasted his methods with those of modern American corporations, where the taking of a meeting is so often an exercise in "postponement" or "deferral," the currently correct terms for "procrastination," "hesitation," and "irresolution."

3. It was rumored that Cole Porter wrote "Don't Fence Me In" as a birthday present for Hamlet. Both men denied the allegation. No shortage of idlers chuckled over the insinuation that the prince was bisexual. See Jacques Plante, *The Invention of the Mask*, chapter two.

where he was among the first to recognize the importance of Stravinsky's *Rite of Spring*. In competition with a cousin, he wrote a sonnet cycle based on a remark Nijinsky made about the ease with which he stayed in the air while leaping.[4]

Back in England Hamlet, a natural toastmaster, took Disraeli's side in his clashes with Gladstone and relished the anecdote that found the pair at a social gathering. Gladstone said to Disraeli, "I predict, Sir, that you will die either by hanging or of some vile disease." Disraeli replied, "That depends, Sir, upon whether I embrace your principles or your mistress." Hamlet's diaries provide abundant evidence that, even at the age of 23, the young man could foresee a time when nostalgia for his early manhood would be unbearably intense. It was this foretaste of nostalgia that impelled him to accept a one-year appointment as a fellow of Trinity College, Cambridge. He had first-floor digs in the Great Court and threw an admirable champagne-and-oysters party in his rooms once a term. Within months he was invited to join the Apostles, the prestigious secret club that listed John Maynard Keynes, E. M. Forster, Rupert Brooke, and Virginia Woolf's husband Leonard among its members. (Hamlet declined, pleading time limitations; but to Horatio he confided his disapproval of the Bloomsbury circle's politics.) When the year was up, he moved to London and lived in a garden flat in Covent Garden. His production of *Ghosts* is still the ideal by which productions of Ibsen are judged.[5] A play he wrote for the Mummers in Cambridge took the form of a debate between Brutus in *Julius Caesar* and Antony in *Antony and Cleopatra*, with the Cleopatra scenes done in the nude. He is said to have had love affairs with Alma Mahler and the young Vivien Leigh.[6]

4. "By the sixth sonnet in the chain, you suspect that the true theme of 'Nijinsky's Leap' is a meditation on being and time. The forest imagery, the dance metaphor, and the peculiarly modern worry that our lives lack authenticity are striking features of the work."—Mary Worthington, *The Guardian*.

5. From E. M. Forster's review (1928): "The symbolism never holds up the action, because it is part of the action, and because [Hamlet is] a poet, to whom creation and craftsmanship [are] one. . . . It is the same with the fire of life in *Ghosts*. . . . Everything rings true and echoes far because it is in the exact place which its surroundings require."

6. He may have been an inspiration to John F. Kennedy, but—notwithstanding rumors to the contrary—he did not share the young president's satyriasis.

Hamlet drank moderately, beer primarily, though there were nights he would treat all patrons to "a butt of sack" in such old-time pubs as the Mistress of Quickly on Cadogan Street, or the Prince of Wales, where he showed flashes of the wit and charm that had made more than one maiden overcome her inhibitions. With his sleepy head in Ophelia's lap, he assumed the countenance of a young cherub but steered the dialogue subtly to country matters. Let's face it, he was a very demanding guy, fickle, self-absorbed, a true prince. Nevertheless he impressed half the world with his martial energy, his jovial hospitality, his biting wit, and his calculated lunacy. There was (Ophelia smiled) method acting in his madness. The sight of Hamlet in fencing gear acted like an aphrodisiac, she added.

Hamlet joined U.S. Army Intelligence after recruitment by General T. J. Evans in February 1945.

It sometimes seems that half of seventeenth-century English poetry is devoted to the love of God and the other half to the pursuit and seduction of a young lady.

Two Poems in the Courtly Manner

1.

Gather ye rosebuds come what may,
Old time's a frequent flyer,
And many lovers that link today
May soon be forced to retire.

Let each of us have one, each of us be one
Soul unlinking from its mate in the past
To eat the golden apples of the sun.
Youth fondly supposes it will last.

Death is what happens to someone else,
The soon-to-be forgotten lad who fell
On the tracks or was pushed by a false
Prophet casting his spell. Let all who fall

Learn how to fail. It may be that death
Is the only subject worthy of our time,
Because at any moment our breath
May cease. But that is no bar to rhyme,

Much less love. And postponement is a sin
If earthly pleasure earns the nod
Of approval that any God worthy of the din
May grant in the temple of our union.

So dance and sing, spread your wings far and wide;
Love when you can, all dreams must end;
Be happy while ye may; and let the lovers ride
Ahead of the field: the happy pair, lover and friend.

2.

Gather ye rosebuds while ye may;
Tomorrow is another day.
Gather ye rosebuds if you must,
And into ashes all my lust.

A sweet disorder in the dress
Befits a damsel in distress.
Wherever my Julia goes
The honey of her beauty flows.

Tell me—for oracles must still ascend,
Knock, breathe, shine and seek to mend—
What tongues of flame are equal to my lust?
Gather ye rosebuds if you must.

A proper haiku has seventeen syllables stretched across three lines in a pattern of five-seven-five. On a visit to Japan in 1990 I translated Bashō's famous haiku as many as two dozen times. The most successful of my efforts does away entirely with the rules and consists of merely three syllables.

Poem in the Manner of Bashō

Pond
Frog
Splash

In Christopher ("Kit") Smart's hands, an homage to his cat Jeoffry could turn into praise of God and all creation. Molly was an Airedale belonging to my friend Glen. The last three lines of the poem include quotations from Samuel Johnson, Walt Whitman, and Christopher Smart.

For I Will Consider Your Dog Molly

—after Christopher Smart

For it was the first day of Rosh Ha'shanah, New Year's Day, day of
  remembrance, of ancient sacrifices and averted calamities.
For I started the day by eating an apple dipped in honey, as ritual
  required.
For I went to the local synagogue to listen to the ram's horn blown.
For I asked Our Father, Our King, to save us for his sake if not for
  ours, for the sake of his abundant mercies, for the sake of his
  right hand, for the sake of those who went through fire and
  water for the sanctification of his name.
For despite the use of a microphone and other gross violations of
  ceremony, I gave myself up gladly to the synagogue's sensual
  insatiable vast womb.
For what right have I to feel offended?
For I communed with my dead father, and a conspicuous tear rolled
  down my right cheek, and there was loud crying inside me.
For I understood how that tear could become an orb.
For the Hebrew melodies comforted me.
For I lost my voice.

For I met a friend who asked "Is this a day of high seriousness," and
when I said yes he said "It has taken your voice away."

For he was right, for I felt the strong lashes of the wind lashing me by
the throat.

For I thought there shall come a day that the watchmen upon the hills
of Ephraim shall cry, Arise and let us go up to Zion unto the
Lord our God.

For the virgin shall rejoice in the dance, and the young and old in each
other's arms, and their soul shall be as a watered garden, and
neither shall they learn war any more.

For God shall lower the price of bread and corn and wine and oil, he
shall let our cry come up to him.

For in my household it was customary on the afternoon of the first day
of Rosh Ha'shanah to cast not bread but a stone into the depths
of the sea, to weep and pray to weep no more.

For the stone represents all the sins of the people.

For I asked you and Molly to accompany me to Cascadilla Creek,
there being no ocean nearby.

For we talked about the Psalms of David along the way, and the story
of Hannah, mother of Samuel, who sought the most robust bard
to remedy her barrenness.

For Isaac said "I see the fire and the wood, but where is the lamb for
the offering?"

For as soon as I saw the stone, white flat oblong and heavy, I knew
that it had summoned me.

For I heard the voice locked inside that stone, for I pictured a dry
wilderness in which, with a wave of my staff, I could command
sweet waters to flow forth from that stone.

For I cast the stone into the stream and watched it sink to the bottom
where dozens of smaller stones, all of them black, gathered
around it.

For the waterfall performed the function of the chorus.

For after the moment of solemnity dissolved, you playfully tossed
Molly into the stream.

For you tossed her three times, and three times she swam back for her
life.

For she shook the water off her body, refreshed.

For you removed the leash from her neck and let her roam freely.

20

For she darted off into the brush and speared a small gray moving
 thing in the neck.

For this was the work of an instant.

For we looked and behold! the small gray thing was a rat.

For Molly had killed the rat with a single efficient bite, in conformance
 with Jewish law.

For I took the rat and cast him into the stream, and both of us
 congratulated Molly.

For now she resumed her noble gait.

For she does not lie awake in the dark and weep for her sins, and
 whine about her condition, and discuss her duty to God.

For I'd as lief pray with your dog Molly as with any man.

For she knows that God is her savior.

My father, who arrived in the United States as a refugee from Hitler's Germany, used to recite this German poem by heart with an uncanny gleam in his eyes. It has often been translated but never, to my mind, satisfactorily.

Goethe's Nightsong

—a translation of Wandrers Nachtlied *(1780)*

Over the hills
Comes the quiet.
Across the treetops
No breeze blows.
Not a sound: even the small
Birds in the woods are quiet.
Just wait: soon you
Will be quiet, too.

Part Two

John Ashbery once told an interviewer that he read Hölderlin when he needed to "kick-start" his imagination. I feel the same way.

Autumn Evening

—after Friedrich Hölderlin

The yellow pears hang in the lake.
Life sinks, grace reigns, sins ripen, and
in the north dies a tree.

A genius took me by the hand and said
the time has not yet come.

Therefore, when the gods get lonely,
a hero will emerge from the bushes
of a summer evening
bearing the first green figs of the season.

For the glory of the gods has lain asleep
too long in the dark
in darkness too long
too long in the dark.

The poets whose lines I lifted for this cento are, in order, John Clare, Shelley, Wordsworth, Blake, Keats, Blake, Shelley, Wordsworth, Coleridge, Keats, Byron, Coleridge, Poe, and Yeats.

Cento: The True Romantics

I hid my love when young till I
Heard the thunder hoarsely laugh,
Heard the skylark warbling in the sky,
For the eye altering alters all.

But with a sweet forgetting,
And a heaven in a wild flower,
The awful shadow of some unseen power
Hath had elsewhere its setting.

I would build that dome in air
And in the icy silence of the tomb,
For the sword outwears its sheath,

And whom I love, I love indeed,
And all I loved, I loved alone,
Ignorant and wanton as the dawn.

When I think of Wordsworth, I link "boy" and "joy" and consider the idea that the growth of a poet's mind could supplant the expulsion from Eden as the subject for an epic poem. Add the poet's sublime egotism and the sense of dignity that he beheld in leech-gatherers and tranquil old men on foot, and you get some of the ambivalence that we who love Wordsworth feel toward the author of *The Prelude* and "Tintern Abbey."

Poem in the Manner of William Wordsworth

I ran with the wind like a boy
in the journey of my solitude
when joy surrounded me like an ocean
I could not stand in but could drown in.

And thus was born my theory of joy
alloyed with fear and more subdued
than a breeze lifting a lone leaf
to a hill of high altitude.

If such a thought were vain,
to me it yet remains the breath
of life itself, greater than grief
and lonelier than a cloudless sky.

Not even—my sister, my life—not
even if death should be thy lot,
would I lose faith that I,

in body bruised but with dignity high,
with visage grim to meet the pains
of sleep, will yet sustain
the never-ending poem of my brain.

I lifted the first line from Lord Byron, whose comic masterpiece, *Don Juan*, is full of opinions and high-spirited rhymes.

On This Day I Do Not Enter
My Sixth-and-Thirtieth Year

—salutations to Lord Byron

When a man has no freedom to fight for at home
When bullshit artists find new goats to defame
When a man would do as the Vandals did in Rome
When a team of fake heroes loses the big game

And the woman applies mascara
And lets her husband's valet watch
When she takes off her blouse and bra
And draws a hot bath and leaves the door unlatched

Then the moon hides behind a throng of clouds
And passengers tell their life stories to strangers
The jet keeps climbing and the music gets too loud
And the man now knows he is addicted to danger

And no glass shows the woman's grief or the man's
And soldiers die lonely and forlorn in foreign lands.

Keats's sonnet on Chapman's Homer was my stimulus here. Keats's first line is "Much have I traveled in the realms of gold." The last word in the poem is "Darien."

Poem in the Manner of John Keats

Much have I trampled among meads of grass,
And many pretty pistils seen,
Round many wakeful tulips been
Where bashful buds appoint the blushing lass.
Her lips with crimson in the looking glass,
Her death-deceiving forehead foreseen:
Yet never met I a maiden more serene
When o'er the green corn field we passed.
Then framed I this memory of her sighs
And sent it to the steward of my pain,
Who spurred me to pen a sonnet to her eyes.
I wondered: will I see her brow again,
Will I hear her whisper and moan
Again, or cry for her life in dire ruin?

The odd fact that both Vermeer and Keats were born on Halloween emboldened me to attempt this "astrological profile" of Keats. It was written for *The Best American Poetry* blog. Something about the immediacy and informality of a blog invites one to risk irreverence.

On Keats's Birthday

—an astrological profile

Poor Keats. A Scorpio with Virgo rising and, just to clinch the deal, his *moon in Gemini.* This is the equivalent of being dealt the Fool, the Lovers (inverted), and the Tower as the three culminating cards in an eleven-card tarot reading. There is sadness in his life, illness, a consumptive cough. But he has a generous soul, he meets afflictions with renewed resolve, he is capable of great feats of self-discipline. Willing to work hours on meters and rhymes, he is a born dreamer, who can shut his eyes and transport himself in a second to fairy lands forlorn, an enchantment of mist, an early autumn of heirloom tomatoes and three varieties of peaches. Life is a struggle, but he prevails, and then dies young.

Born on the 31st of October, Keats had a soft spot for Halloween and tried his hand at writing spooky verses that would scare school chums sitting around the campfire during the season of burning leaves. The fact that his moon is in Gemini, that the nocturnal northeastern quadrant is predominant in his natal chart, and above all that Mercury is his ruling planet, supports the view of this poet as a divinely ordained messenger of the gods trapped in the frail body of an undernourished

London lad with his face pressed against the sweet shop window, as Yeats wrote.[1]

Keats's Venus is, like his sun, in Scorpio. This is crucial. It means he is as passionate as he is sensitive and a gambler not by instinct or by social association but by his intransigent attachment to his ideals. He can be loved by many but reserves his own love for one. Auden's poem "The More Loving One" depicts a conflict that Keats resolved each time he picked up his pen to write. He felt he was destined to be the more loving one in any partnership, and he would not have had it any other way, but he didn't live long enough to test his resolve.

Keats loved the four elements and presented their interplay with the clarity that Vermeer brought to the study of light. (Vermeer, too, was born on Halloween.) In an unpublished story by E. M. Forster with a strong hint of bisexuality and a blithe disregard of historical possibility, the seventeenth-century Vermeer and the nineteenth-century Keats—accompanied by Dorothy Wordsworth (nineteenth century) and Virginia Woolf (twentieth century)—meet in Oxford and discuss aesthetics and metaphysics as they float slowly down the Cherwell on a punt.

The story that Keats died because of a bad review in an influential Edinburgh journal is to the biography of English poets what history was in the mind of the automobile manufacturer who invented the assembly line, bunk, but it was kept fresh by Byron's oft-quoted couplet in *Don Juan*: "'Tis strange the mind, that very fiery particle / Should let itself be snuff'd out by an article." The mischievous Byron, born on January 22 (1788)—an Aquarius trailing clouds of Capricorn, and with Cancer as his rising sign—was as conflicted on the subject of his younger Cockney-born contemporary as Emerson was about Whitman after the former praised the latter, who proceeded to enlarge *Leaves of Grass* almost beyond recognition.

The position of Mercury in the third house has caused the greatest

1. If you mix up the names Keats and Yeats, or pronounce one as if it were the other, the chances of your appreciating either are diminished but not eliminated. The two names are separated by nearly five decades but linked by lyrical genius, with the prophetic mode ascendant in Yeats, while Keats—brainy, anxious, and quick as befits a son of Mercury—wins the laurels for sensuality and freshness: the palpable bubbles in the wineglass, the burst of a grape in the satyr's mouth, the humming of flies on the porch screen in August, keen fitful gusts of wind.

amount of comment among professional astrologers. The consensus view is that Keats resembled certain musical geniuses in his extraordinary talent, his humble origins, and his early death. Though he was less dashing than the noble Byron and less angelic of aspect than Shelley, all the women polled said they would welcome a relationship with Keats, especially if she is in England while he is in Italy writing long gorgeous letters to her about Shakespeare plays, the nature of inspiration, the smell of mortality, and what Adam felt like waking up in Eden. Keats proved that greatness descends on the novice only after he has opened himself up to the risk of failure or embarrassment.

The muse visited Keats often in the spring of 1819. First came "The Eve of St. Agnes," the lovers rushing away into the night; then "La Belle Dame Sans Merci," the lover seduced and abandoned. These poems were as immediate as dreams. And then came the odes, the greatest odes that English has to offer: to Psyche, to a Nightingale, on a Grecian Urn, on Melancholy, to Indolence. No poet ever packed as much magnificence in a line or wrote stanzas of such melodious charm that a simple, naive statement of Platonic optimism, which in lesser hands would be anticlimactic or worse, should seem to penetrate the heart of the mystery: "Beauty is Truth, Truth Beauty."

(October 31, 2012)

I read Whitman in high school and immediately wrote poems
with long lines and the voice of a chest-thumping American bard.
The danger of imitating the "barbaric yawp" is mitigated by the
reminder that in many ways Whitman came along as if in fulfill-
ment of a prophecy made by Ralph Waldo Emerson, who is para-
phrased at the end of this effort.

Poem in the Manner of Walt Whitman

Last night I walked among the gray-faced onanists and the women
    who love unrequited.
I saw the blind, heard the deaf, smelled the alcohol on their breath,
    tasted the sweat on the neck of a wounded man, and O I walked
    all the night long and I knew.
Each one sleeps, some faster than others, some more skillfully
    navigating in the dark, others snoring in the ears of their patient
    wives, some in noun clusters, others in sentences that daybreak
    will disperse.
Each one dreams, the woman who paints her face, the loiterer, the
    shoplifter, the trombonist on his way to the cellar bar, the
    prisoner who knows he is guiltless.
They may sleep wearing clothes, pajamas or a slip, or even perhaps a
    cotton T-shirt, but they dream in the nakedness of the night.
I have watched the father watching his son outgrow him and I have
    seen the daughter take her mother's place.
The boy who stutters, I watch him sleep, I hear him dream, and I see
    him become a man of means and distinction.
The shopkeeper, the beggar, the young policeman affecting

nonchalance, the drunkard asleep, the woman with the painted
    face walking under the overpass,
I see them fade in the night, into the same darkness that receives me,
    and the endless yammering of philosophers I hear,
Each one contradicting the other, each quoting some sage of antiquity,
And if I could make them understand that I rejoice in their right to
    exist
Yet would not, were they to knock on my door, welcome them inside,
Nor grieve to learn that they have moved to Montana,
I would sleep contented in the dreamless zone before dawn.

For all intents and purposes, Baudelaire invented the prose poem, a form that seemed ultra new when I read Rimbaud as a college freshman. One mode favored by Baudelaire was the truncated story that climaxes in an unexpected epiphany.

Poem in the Manner of Charles Baudelaire

The task of painting and installing a door is a charming respite for a soul fatigued from the struggles of life. The quality of the wood, the choice of the color, the need for precise measurements: all these things absorb him. And then there are the spectral presences that have followed him noiselessly throughout the day and attend him even now, and with whom he holds lively if silent discourse while affixing the door with its hinges to the portal. The woman for whom he has built this door has opened a bottle of red wine and transferred its contents to a shapely flask. The perfume enters the air where it takes the form of quarter notes. There are flowers in a vase on the piano. All this the carpenter sees, and by the time he has installed the door, sweaty and in need of a shower, he sees that the woman has shed her outer garments, and is staring at him with a look alternately frank and coy, and his penis springs to an erection like the salute of a well-trained soldier, and his soul enjoys that mysterious and aristocratic pleasure reserved for the man of action who wins a decoration for steadfastness of purpose and steadiness of aim.

Baudelaire took Poe's concept of the "imp of the perverse" and raised it to an aesthetic ideal.

Let's Beat Up Some Beggars!

—a translation of Baudelaire's Assomons les pauvres!

For two full weeks I stayed in my room, surrounded by the fashionable books of the day (this was sixteen or seventeen years ago); I mean the genre of books that teach people how to be happy, gain wisdom, and get rich, all within twenty-four hours. I had thus digested—I should say swallowed—all the lucubrations of all the entrepreneurs of public happiness—including those who would advise the poor to become slaves and those who would persuade them that they are all dethroned kings. Unsurprisingly I emerged from this regimen in a dizzy state of consciousness, a dazed stupor.

It seemed to me that I had, in the depths of my mind, the nugget of an idea greater than all the old-wives' formulas that I had recently studied. But it was only the idea of an idea, something infinitely vague.

And I left the house with a mighty thirst. A passion for bad books creates a corresponding craving for refreshments and the open air.

As I was about to enter a bar, a beggar presented his hat to me, giving me one of those unforgettable looks that would overthrow the government if spirit could move matter and if the eyes of a hypnotist could ripen grapes.

At the same time, I heard a voice whispering in my ear, a voice that I knew well; it was that of the good Angel, or good Demon, that accompanies me wherever I go. Since Socrates had his good Demon, why should I not have my good Angel, why should I not have the honor, like Socrates, to earn my own certificate of folly, signed by the subtle Lelut and the shrewd Baillarger?[1]

There exists this difference between Socrates' demon and mine: his appeared only to defend, warn, or constrain him while mine advises, suggests, encourages. Poor Socrates had a forbidding demon; mine is greatly affirmative, a Demon of action, a Demon of combat.

Now the voice in my ear whispered: "A man is equal to another only if he proves it, and he alone deserves his liberty who knows how to win it."

I promptly turned on my beggar. With one punch, I closed one of his eyes, which instantly grew as large as a ball. I split a fingernail knocking out two of his teeth, and because I am not the strongest of men, with a delicate constitution from birth and with precious little practice at boxing, I thought I would finish off the old man by seizing his coat collar with one hand, his throat with the other, and then banging his head hard against the wall. I freely admit that before taking action I had scoped out the area and made sure that in this deserted suburb I was, for the time being, beyond the purview of the police.

Having kicked his back hard enough to bust his shoulder blades, I knocked down the feeble sexagenarian, then picked up a branch lying on the ground and used the stick to beat him with the gusto of a chef pounding a steak to make it tender.

Suddenly—O miracle! O joy of the philosopher who proves his theory valid!—I saw that ancient carcass return to life, getting up with a bounce that I would never have expected in so decrepit a body. With a look of hate that struck me as most promising, this fossil threw himself at me, blackened both my eyes, broke four of my teeth, and with the self-same stick I had used, beat me to a pulp.—Through my vigorous treatment, I had restored his pride and his life.

At this point I signaled to him that I considered the discussion closed. And with the satisfaction of a Sophist of the painted portico in Athens, I got up and said to him: "Sir, *you are my equal!* Do me the honor of sharing my purse; and remember, if you love your fellow man, that you must apply to all your brethren, when they beseech you for alms, the theory that I have had the *sorrow* to test on your back."

He swore that he grasped the theory and would heed my counsel.

1. Baillarger, Lelut: noted psychiatrists in nineteenth-century France.

Emily Dickinson's terseness and use of dash marks are as inviting as her ability to render aspects of experience—an afterlife, for example—that defy the rational intellect.

Poem in the Manner of Emily Dickinson

Paradise—

(c. 1886)

Thomas Hardy's pessimism, expressed in a homely manner disdainful of grand gestures, made a major impression on modern British poets from Auden to Larkin. I wrote this parody in self-defense.

The Hapless Hour

—after Thomas Hardy

There comes a time in the life of God
(Presuming He exists) when He
(Or She, or It, as the case may be)
Lets loose with a laugh at me that sod

Is destined to cover (if, of course,
I am thought about at all). No doubt
A bird will mark the hour, and out
Of his puny chest will come a hoarse

And puny voice, resigned to go unheard,
Unheeded. In early March, at break
Of dusk it will happen. Just as I

Prepare to say goodbye, the bird
Will drop a turd, as if by mistake.
There is no justice in the winter sky.

With his emphatic alliteration and his heavily accented verse, Hopkins proves that the theme of religion and the idea of divinity can retain their validity in a godless age.

Poem in the Manner of Gerard Manley Hopkins

I went this morning to mourn
the morning I never see
as the rude sailor's red sky warns
the rood-recking rookie
(man of, mad of, masts and mists and myths)
for first time facing strange seas
as fast as flames and as fatal to moths,
and all things private, princely in sloth.

As the sea with long-lived weeds looks
to blinded-with-blond-sun boys in books,
so eyes see inward with a flicker or flash,
and all things clamor, each with the glamour
of flame flinging wood or wings to ash:
and all things private, corporal, major mourn.

As a freshman at Columbia I stumbled upon Rimbaud's *Illuminations*, prose poems that arrested me with their associative logic, the way they leap from one fragmented insight to another. The experience reinforced the lesson that the enjoyment of great poetry precedes the comprehension of it.

Poem in the Manner of Arthur Rimbaud

Wandering in the forest I was naked as the dawn that has never before seen herself naked. But no bell tolled and no cock crowed.

Between the waterfall and the wall stood the incautious girls of my village, which I left when I reached my fifteenth birthday, fed up with the bitches picked up in cafés who would have me own what I preferred to possess by short-term lease.

A troupe of actors met me in a clearing. They lent me my costume, taught me their song and dance, introduced me to their queen, and fed me bread and wine.

"I tell you, she is the queen of all France," I said, and she blushed, the most provincial of three royal sisters.

We made love in the clearing but we called it fucking.

And when I was hungry and thirsty a bird directed me back to a village of bells and a tall clock tower with five different clock faces, each telling the same minute but a different hour accurate somewhere in the world.

Part Three

As a believer in ad hoc poetic forms, I hold a brief for the multiple-choice test—a form with which nearly everyone is familiar. The multiplicity of options allows not only for truths and facts but also for a variety of fictions, tonalities, ironies, humor.

Freud Quiz

Freud Quiz #1

Freud in German means
(a) Fright
(b) Joy
(c) Sautéed lightly with olive oil
(d) "The young eagle, a rank impostor, fled the Reich."
(e) The same thing "it" means in German.[1]
(f) The fourth movement of Beethoven's Ninth

1. "I would guess (e) because of the quote marks. My reasoning: It is obvious that Freud is greater than the sum of his disciples (d), and I would argue that (a) is archaic, and (b) is accurate only if one approves of Beethoven's translation of Schiller (f). So that leaves (c) and (e), and the former is too great a concession to the spirit of camp. The real question is whether 'it' is (1) the id, (2) Freud as a proper noun, i.e., a signifier with surplus meaning, or (3) the universal pronoun."
    —John Casebeer

Freud Quiz #2

According to Freud in *The Future of an Illusion*, what is an illusion?
(a) A falsehood.
(b) Something that may be true or may come true but probably won't.
(c) Religion.
(d) Art.
(e) A ghost in the sense intended by Ibsen in his play *Ghosts*.[2]

Freud Quiz #3

What does "beyond the pleasure principle" refer to?
(a) A book by Sigmund Freud.
(b) A vast right-wing conspiracy.
(c) Death.
(d) The dark side of the moon considered as an image for female
    sexuality.
(e) The sadness following orgasm.
(f) The unconscious.
(g) The desire to retreat into the womb.
(h) The heroine's disastrous first marriage.

Freud Quiz #4

Freud came up with great titles, which poets like to steal, and the best
    of these is
(a) *The Interpretation of Dreams*
(b) *Jokes and Their Relation to the Unconscious*
(c) *Civilization and Its Discontents*
(d) *The Problem of Anxiety*
(e) *Totem and Taboo*

2. "This is the summation of the play," Tertan said. "Everything seemed to turn upon duty and I am afraid I made your poor father's home unbearable to him, Oswald.' Spoken by Mrs. Alving." Cf. Joseph Howe, *Life and Letters* (1943).

Freud Quiz #5

What is the "compulsion to repeat"?
(a) the impulse to keep doing the thing that scares you—in an effort to master the fear
(b) the reason why Hitler copied Napoleon's disastrous invasion of Russia
(c) the need to repeat the same futile action and the madness of expecting a different result
(d) the belief that history doesn't repeat itself but it sometimes rhymes[3]
(e) voting for candidates named Kennedy, Clinton, or Bush

Freud Quiz #6

Psychoanalysis became known as the "talking cure" because
(a) it depends on free association
(b) all talk and no action make Jack a dull boy
(c) it was the talk of Viennese café society
(d) he heard a woman's voice in a dream: "she'll be riding six white horses when she comes." And he woke up feeling pretty good.[4]
(e) the shrink with the hearing aid is the single greatest metaphor for the profession since Groucho Marx told a mother of eight that he liked his cigar a lot but took it out of his mouth once in a while, and the conversation went on from there.
(f) a session was like a church confessional

Freud Quiz #7

In Freud's view, when the Dalai Lama met Salvador Dalí
(a) They discussed a possible merger of Surrealism and Buddhism.

3. When this statement, sometimes attributed to Mark Twain, was mentioned to Elizabeth Arden, she replied, "Repetition makes reputation and reputation makes customers," which quickly became a merchandising mantra.
4. Compare the last line of Philip Roth's *Portnoy's Complaint* with that of Norman Mailer's *The Naked and the Dead*.

(b) They criticized U.S. foreign policy.

(c) They were in a Gap commercial for khaki trousers.

(d) They sang "Hello, Dolly."

(e) It was like the meeting of an umbrella and a sewing machine on an operating table.

Freud Quiz #8[5]

If Jacques Lacan had written *Beyond the Pleasure Principle*, death would be

a) A one-way ticket to Palookaville

b) The big sleep

c) A modern office building

d) A seventeenth-century orgasm

e) The mirror

Freud Quiz #9

1. Who wrote the *Confessions* of Rousseau?
2. Who wrote *The Confessions of Nat Turner*?
3. Who wrote the *Confessions of a Justified Sinner*?
4. Who wrote *The Autobiography of Alice B. Toklas*?
5. Who played Boswell to Samuel Johnson?

Freud Quiz #10

Freud, an avowed agnostic, said that he remained culturally Jewish. The best evidence for this is

(a) the skullcap that he wore when having sex with his wife

(b) in no photograph do you ever see Freud smile

(c) Freud compiled a joke book as diligently as he collected dreams and errors

5. "Freud Quiz" is supported by a grant from the tomb.

(d) he refused to take a Rorschach Test
(e) he left Vienna for London rather than die at the hands of the Nazis

Freud Quiz #11

Freud maintained that death was
(a) the best of a bad business
(b) the best of both worlds
(c) the right answer
(d) one of two unknowns in the equation
(e) the greater of two evils

Bonus points: Auden concludes his elegy for Freud by saying, "sad is Eros, builder of cities, / and weeping anarchic Aphrodite." What makes Auden call Eros—the impish god of love, known in Latin as Cupid— "builder of cities"?

Freud Quiz #12

At which of these jokes did Freud laugh:
(a) "Catholic is to wholesale as Protestant is to retail."
(b) "A wife is like an umbrella. Sooner or later you take a cab."
(c) "This girl is like Dreyfus. The army doesn't believe in her innocence."
(d) "Was your mother once in service at the palace?" "No, your Highness, but my father was."
(e) Blind man: "*Wie gehts?*" Lame man: "As you see."

Freud Quiz #13

What do women want?
(a) what they have
(b) what they don't have
(c) a cigar

(d) R-E-S-P-E-C-T

(e) next question

Freud Quiz #14

Freud's discovery of "drives" came about because
(a) some dreams cannot be ascribed to wish fulfillment.
(b) when Freud played golf in Scotland, he favored drivers over putters
(c) he was inspired by the Walter Donaldson song "You're Driving Me
      Crazy"
(d) there was no better way to account for the animal attraction between
      the sexes, which would otherwise exist in strict opposition
(e) there was no other way to explain death.

Freud Quiz #15

When John Huston made a movie of Freud's life, whom did he cast in
      the part of the Viennese father of psychoanalysis?
a) John Huston's own father, Walter
b) George Montgomery
c) Montgomery Clift
d) Huston never made a movie of Freud's life
e) Anthony Perkins in fright wig
f) Susanna York

Freud Quiz #16

In addition to John Huston's *Freud*, which of these movies deals with
      the papa of psychoanalysis:
(1) Orson Welles's *The Trial* in which Joseph K. (Anthony Perkins)—
      and by extension Kafka himself—is understood to be Freud's
      anti-type and thus, by Freudian logic, Freud himself.
(2) Orson Welles's *Chimes at Midnight* in which Freud disguised as
      Falstaff (Orson Welles) cavorts after hours with tippling cronies
      and good-natured prostitutes.

(3) Kurosawa's *Throne of Blood* in which Freud is depicted as a
    version of Macbeth, with Mrs. Freud (Lady Macbeth) providing
    the brains and the drive of the operation.
(4) Hitchcock's *Spellbound* in which Gregory Peck is an amnesiac,
    Ingrid Bergman is his analyst, and Freud is Ingrid Bergman's
    father in upstate New York.
(5) Sam Peckinpah's *The Wild Bunch*, an allegory about the triumph
    of Freud's ego psychology (William Holden) over rival theories
    of the universe such as those of Karl Marx (the Mexicans),
    Lenin (the machine gun), and Jacques Derrida (the scorpions).
    Ernest Borgnine plays Freud's wife and Robert Ryan is Jung.
    Also starring Ben Johnson as his brother and Warren Oates
    as himself. Holden (giving an order): "Let's go." Oates: "Why
    not?" For extra credit, what is the last thing Holden says in the
    movie?

Freud Quiz #17

In what movie does a murder suspect tell a bearded, benevolent
    psychoanalyst, "Freud is hooey"?
Clues:
"Women make the best analysts until they get married. Then they
    make the best patients."
The seven of clubs.
She is glad he didn't dream of her as an eggbeater, as another of her
    patients had done.
"Any husband of Constance is a husband of mine."
The proprietor had a small wheel in his hand.
The hero registered as John Brown in the hotel.

Freud Quiz #18

The reason you never see Freud smiling in a photograph is
a) he kept a straight face at all times
b) he refused to smile on command

c) Viennese professors took pride in their solemnity
d) psychoanalysis was a joke, but he didn't want to give the game
    away
e) photography was still in its infancy

Freud Quiz #19

The stated agenda of *Moses and Monotheism* is
(a) Moses was an Egyptian.
(b) Monotheism was an advance on polytheism because the
    concentration of divinity in a single entity meant that man
    could solve for equations with two unknowns in elementary
    algebra.
(c) Moses went to the wilderness in a vain effort to account for his
    identity.
(d) Peace in the Middle East.
(e) Moses was a woman.

Freud Quiz #20

To explain how man acquired the power of fire, Freud appeals to
    which of the following:
(1) The story of Prometheus, the Titan, who stole the fire of the
    gods and gave it, hidden in a phallic-shaped hollow rod, to
    humankind. For this crime he was punished most vilely: each
    day a vulture feasted on his liver, which in ancient times was
    regarded as the seat of all passion and desires.
(2) The organ that Heine describes in these lines: "*Was dem Menschen
    dient zum Seichen, / Damit schafft er seinesgleichen.*" ["With
    that which serves a man to piss / He reproduces his kind
    and fathers his kids."] The child thinks he can do both
    things at once. But the adult knows that "the two acts are as
    incompatible as fire and water."
(3) The fact that the penis is sometimes in a fiery state of excitation
    that justifies calling it a cock in English (or a *Vogel*, or bird, in
    German). In such a state, urination is impossible.

(4) The example of fictional characters such as Gargantua and Pantagruel in Rabelais and Gulliver in Swift, who put out fires by pissing on them, dramatizing that such an action is natural and instinctive and must be renounced by mankind if we are going to achieve civilization and its attendant discontents.

(5) Hercules can achieve his triumph over the hydra-headed water snake of Lerna only when he uses fire to burn out the snake's one immortal head—which seems counter to the thrust of our argument until we "reverse the manifest content."

Freud Quiz #21

A Freudian slip is

(a) A courteous form letter from *The New Yorker* declining to print your latest effort "despite its obvious merit."

(b) A patch of a woman's white slip strategically exposed beneath her skirt or dress.

(c) The inability to keep a secret, usually but not always sexual.

(d) The laughter aroused when a rotund man slips on a banana peel and flies spectacularly to a hard landing on the pavement.

(e) A mistake attributable to deep subconscious elements in the human psyche.

(f) An error, as in the joke Jung told Freud about the man, the woman, and the duck entering a bar, which resulted in Jung's expulsion from the movement on the grounds that either "woman" or "duck" was code for "Jew" in that joke.[6]

(g) A pyrrhic victory, or déjà vu in French.

Freud Quiz #22

One August day in 1909 Freud fainted in Jung's company because
(1) He was eating lunch and the schnitzel disagreed with him.

6. A pig figures in the joke but in a purely rhetorical sense. "If you tell an animal joke, your chances of getting a laugh will improve if you make the animal a duck," Jack Benny told an interviewer.

(2) He felt a sexual attraction to Jung.

(3) Freud had slept with his wife's younger sister and Jung threatened to blackmail him after hearing him talk about it in his sleep on the trip the two men took to America.

(4) They were having an argument about something trivial when Jung revealed himself to be a virulent anti-Semite. "You're next," he said with an evil laugh. He kept repeating, *"Jude Jude Jude."*

(5) Either Freud said the father of monotheism must have hated his own father and Jung gave him a dirty look, or Jung told Freud the joke about the man, the woman, and the duck entering a bar.

(6) Jung said the spring weather made him feel like a young man. From this innocuous remark, Freud knew that Jung was an impostor. "You were never Jung!" Freud cried.

Freud Quiz #23

Where did Freud and Dante hold their first summit meeting?
(a) The Sands Hotel in Las Vegas, 1962
(b) The Minetta Tavern in Greenwich Village
(c) With Ulysses and Diomedes in the Eighth Circle of *The Inferno*
(d) Stanza 14 of Auden's elegy for Freud
(e) Omaha Beach on June 6, 1944
(f) AA
(e) In New York City's war on crime

Freud Quiz #24

Where and when did Freud die, and of what cause?
(1) At Freiberg (then part of Moravia) of a gunshot wound said to be self-inflicted on 6 May 1856
(2) In London of throat cancer on 23 September 1939
(3) Brokenhearted in North London of so-called natural causes on 14 March 1883
(4) In Paris, executed by guillotine, 28 July 1794

(5) In the saddle on 26 January 1979

(6) Of food poisoning a week after the publication of *Traumdeutung* in Vienna on 1 November 1899

Freud Quiz #25:

What were Freud's last words?

(1) *Mehr licht! Mehr licht!*

(2) More beer!

(3) Either the wallpaper goes, or I do.

(4) Friends, applaud! The comedy is finished.

(5) Don't let it end like this. Tell them I said something.

(6) Am I dying or is it my birthday?

Cavafy wrote about sexual relationships, longing, and homoerotic desire with unparalleled warmth, candor, and sensuality.

Poem in the Manner of C. P. Cavafy

The room had a bed with torn sheets
above the bar where I met her
on Tuesdays in June and July.
And the light was bad, and there were
holes in the screens in the windows
where flies and mosquitoes
came in with the heat
and the laughter of the workers
playing poker downstairs.

And in that narrow room stinking
of cigarette smoke I breathed in
the bliss that only the young
and invincible know when
her young breasts rose and pressed
against my chest, and I was drunk
on her kisses and all these years later
I am drunk again though alone
as I think of those nights with her.

It is difficult to assimilate Yeats's influence. Theodore Roethke and John Berryman were among the estimable poets whom Yeats's example seemed to thwart. But the Irish poet's use of masks, his phrase-making, and his chimes are hard to resist.

Poem in the Manner of William Butler Yeats

Now as at all times I wear his ancient mask
and walk alone in the lofty way of one
who, with the cold courtesy of fishermen
in trout-besotted streams, meets the dawn.
And now they are gone, never to return;
and now who will sing of their innocence,
swing the censer, light a fire, and burn
with passion deep for poetry and dance?
From the ruby throat of a hummingbird
I hear the question you left unasked.
Who would rejoice in the power of ignorance
and walk with his maker and an unnamed third?
Who but a paltry man wearing a public mask,
observing instead of joining in the dance?

As a graduate student in England, homesick for the American language, I read Gertrude Stein's lectures and her *Tender Buttons* and felt immediately heartened. No one has gone beyond Stein in experimentation with grammar and syntax, though many have tried.

Poem in the Manner of Gertrude Stein

A knife near a lemon near a glass any time there is a pin there are one two or nine or ten and open all and then you have it. You have it then and not an apron nor a pot of glue you have it and no other car no car of rouge no glass will do. A dress is not a hairdo. A nip in time is not a mile not the lime on top of the pot or the smile along the mile-long sedge on the river's edge. Tip red slipper white slipper red Joe. Tip black stop white let go no go. From the red to the black no go no luck no lack. A song. A sign. You use it to sue. The psychic was chic, but not too, as mother laughter guides her other daughter to the father slaughter. Nowhere? Now, here. Not a ton but a tub, "and DNA."

If you like walking alone in the woods, as I do, you might read "Birches" and "The Wood-Pile" and "Design," admire the poet's ability to reconcile folksy idiom with traditional metrical pattern, and then see how his vision of things modifies your experience the next time you sit down to compose a poem.

Poem in the Manner of Robert Frost

When I think of walking in a pathless forest,
bleeding from skin wounds inflicted by thorns,
and life is a matter of walking along, without rest,
I walk and watch the birds being born.

Like other walkers I sometimes look
down at the ground not up at the sky.
Insects mate in a brook.
A spider chews a fly.

But when you watch a bird being born,
you know the rest of your life will be dying.
The rest of the night is a sleepless morn.
You are dying to live, and you live by dying.

And when from the woods you emerge
a free man once more,
in your heart you still can feel a surge
of fear as loud as a waterfall's roar.

Rilke—whom W. H. Auden called "the Santa Claus of loneliness"—was working on his *Duino Elegies* in 1922. The *Sonnets to Orpheus* occurred to him as a sudden unanticipated interruption. They have a particular power owing to the formal restraints of the sonnet. And the sublime remains near to one who has made a hermitage out of his life.

Poem in the Manner of Rainer Maria Rilke

Far are the moons of Jupiter—yet how much farther
The distance from the boy's bedroom to the hill.
He will fly; he will fall; but he will not fail his father.
Mothers are kind but against free will.

Fate spans the sciences, and perhaps there are many.
But there is one art only, and muses are cruel.
They part with poems as a miser parts with money.
No masters teach the trade to kids in school.

Everything fair is far, and circles are incomplete.
For her he would enlarge the realm of the rose,
For her endure the threat of violence.

At the far end of night will watchmen repeat
The litany of the disenchanted, or—who knows—
Hear a voice when there is no voice but silence?

In the last two lines of Max Jacob's seemingly frivolous "do you know?" poem, the poet claims to be all the people he has just named—even though he is nothing more than a baboon ("*qui ne suis pourtant qu'un babouin*"). Larry Fagin has a version of Jacob's poem peopled with a New York School cast. My version is rhyme-driven.

Poem in the Manner of Max Jacob

Do you know the poems of Max Jacob?
Do you know Talese, Gay? Swenson, May?
Do you know *Goldfinger*, alias Gert Frobe?
Do you know Robinson, Sugar Ray?

Do you know the way to San Jose?
Have you sung with Doris Day?
Have you danced with Danny Kaye?
Do you know the former Cassius Clay?

Have you met Barbara Stanwyck?
Had tea with Henry Kissinger?
Debra Winger? Marlene Dietrich?
Now do you wonder who's kissing her?

Have you taken a selfie with Anita O'Day?
Fay Wray? Zane Grey? Gatsby, Jay?
What about the stories of E. Hemingway?
Have you listened to the music of Billy May?

We little know the ones we would adore
But I'm pretty sure I shall meet them soon
Being all these people myself (and more),
Who am yet only a baboon.

In my college years and for several decades after, Wallace Stevens was the poet laureate of the baccalaureate—the favorite of professors, perhaps because he proposed that in the absence of a divinity, the imagination was "supreme." The logic made existence itself seem an aesthetic proposition.

Poem in the Manner of Wallace Stevens

Not until the days of unrelenting sky,
the water cool, the lily pads on the pond
green with the slime of the deep, did I

note the versions of sea that compound
a surface of blue with the white of foam
or a white bird leaving its native home

that may not exist in an icy haze
if winter comes and, with a boy's courage,
a man walks alone on the shore

between the early yellow of an old marriage
and his first idea of that leafless world,
that giant's view of night's midwinter blaze

where a man and a woman might walk,
might talk, yet neither says a word,
or no one's there except that white bird.

Stevens delighted in his titles: "Someone Puts a Pineapple Together," "Peter Quince at the Clavier," "Le Monocle de Mon Oncle." The title here generated a meditation on the Hartford insurance man who wrote majestic poems in his head while walking to and from his office.

The Matador of Metaphor

—after Wallace Stevens

The grapefruit in the tropical orchard
has ripened into a globe in Hartford
for him to look at, not to eat.
If he had a tin can he would beat
it as a drummer in a band beats
his drum and steadily with a swish
and sometimes a gong. It's his wish
to escape from gray walls and sky
into a Denmark of the inner eye
or a bullring south of the border
or a sky espied from the trenches
of a battlefield in Flanders. Wenches
wander into his wonderland. Order
is disorder squared. We are nowhere
else but here, yet live we do in metaphor
like that elegant square-shouldered matador.

The Stevens poem I was reading was "Re-Statement of Romance" from his book *Ideas of Order.*

Poem in the Manner of Wallace Stevens as Rewritten by Gertrude Stein

If night were not night but the absence of night
an event but not the same event twice then I would be I
and this would be nice very nice as I write I write

you down you write me back I write you a letter you write
me one better and there go you and here come I
where you and I may meet may fight but here there is no night

and I see you see me and if then better than if one might
if one white had struck all yellow and blue and black and green
and all rolled into a ball of white yet here there is no night

here you read the letter as written not the night
as performed and this would be nice you and I and nothing between
the same event twice a ball of white as I write I write

When I lived in Paris as a young man, Apollinaire's "Zone" was my favorite poem. I knew parts of it by heart and would recite them on my daily walks. The celebrated last line, "*soleil cou coupé*," contains a brilliant piece of wordplay that resists the translator's craft. It's as if *cou* (meaning "neck") is an abbreviated form of *coupé* (meaning "cut"). The relation between the two words can be said to suggest the action of the sun rising at dawn and appearing as if beheaded by the horizon. The verse has been variously translated as "Decapitated sun—" (William Meredith), "The sun a severed neck" (Roger Shattuck), "Sun corseless head" (Samuel Beckett), "Sun slit throat" (Anne Hyde Greet), "Sun neck cut" (Charlotte Mandell). Ron Padgett's "Sun cut throat" cleverly divides the word "cutthroat" in two. I have opted for "Let the sun beheaded be," mainly because of the repetition of sounds in the last words. I felt that the relation of "be" to "beheaded" approximated the action in "*cou coupé.*"

Zone

—*a translation of the poem by Guillaume Apollinaire*

In the end you've had enough of the ancient world

O Eiffel Tower shepherdess today your bridges are a bleating flock

You've had it up to here with the Romans and Greeks

Here even the automobiles look antique
Only religion remains new religion
Retains the simplicity of an airport hangar

Alone in Europe you are not antiquated O Christianity
The most modern man in Europe is you Pope Pius X
While you whom the windows watch are too ashamed
To enter a church and confess your sins today
You read handouts pamphlets posters sing to you from up high
There's your morning poetry and for prose there are the newspapers
Paperback police thrillers for twenty-five centimes
Portraits of the great a thousand and one titles

This morning I saw a pretty little street whose name I forget
Clean and new it seemed the clarion of the sun
Executives workers and beautiful stenographers
Pass this way four times a day from Monday morning to Saturday
        night
Three times each morning a siren whines
An angry bell at noon
Billboards signs and murals
Shriek like parakeets
I love the grace of this industrial street
In Paris between the rue Aumont-Thiéville and the avenue des Ternes

Look how young the street is and you still only a toddler
Your mother dresses you in blue and white
You are very religious you and your old pal René Dalize
You love nothing more than church ceremonies
It's nine o'clock the gas turns blue you sneak out of the dormitory
You stay up all night praying in the school chapel
Under a globed amethyst worthy of adoration
The halo around the head of Christ revolves forever
He is the lovely lily that we cultivate
The red-haired torch immune to any wind
The pale and scarlet son of the mother of many sorrows
The evergreen tree ever hung with prayers
The twin gallows of honor and eternity

The six-pointed star
God who dies on Friday and revives on Sunday
Christ who climbs heavens higher than any aviator can reach
He holds the world's aviation record

Christ pupil of my eye
Pupil of twenty centuries he knows what he's doing
And changed into a bird this century like Jesus soars in the air
Devils in abysses lift their heads to stare
Look they say he takes after Simon Magus of Judea
They say he can steal but can also steal away
The angels vault past the all-time greatest pole vaulters
Icarus Enoch Elijah Apollonius of Tyana
Gather around the first airplane
Or make way for the elevation of those who took communion
The priests rise eternally as they raise the host
And the airplane touches down at last its wings outstretched
From heaven come flying millions of swallows
Ibises flamingoes storks from Africa
The fabled roc celebrated by storytellers and poets
With Adam's skull in its claws the original skull
Messenger from the horizon the eagle swoops and screams
And from America the little hummingbird
From China the long and supple pihis
Who have one wing each and fly in pairs
Here comes the dove immaculate spirit
Escorted by lyrebird and vain peacock
And the phoenix engendering himself from the flames
Veils everything for a moment with his sparkling cinders
The sirens leave the perilous seas
And sing beautifully when they get here all three of them
And all of them eagle phoenix and pihi of China
Befriend our flying machine

Now you are walking in Paris all alone among the crowds
Herds of bellowing buses roll by you
Love's anguish grips you by the throat
As if you were fated never again to be loved

In the bad old days you would have entered a monastery
You feel ashamed when you slip and catch yourself saying prayers
You mock yourself your laughter crackles like hellfire
The sparks flash in the depths of your life
Which is a painting hung in a gloomy museum
And sometimes you've got to get as close to it as you can

Today as you walk around Paris and her bloodstained women
It was (and I would just as soon not remember it was) the demise of
     beauty

Surrounded by flames our Lady looked down on me at Chartres
The blood of thy sacred heart drowned me in Montmartre
I am sick of hearing the blessed words
The love I suffer from is a shameful disease
And my image of you survives in my anguish and insomnia
It's always near you and then it fades away

Now you're at the Mediterranean shore
Under the lemon groves in flower all year long
You go sailing with your friends
One is from Nice one from Menton two Turbiasques
The creatures of the deep terrify us
The fish swimming through seaweed is the symbol of our Savior

You're in the garden of a tavern on the outskirts of Prague
You're in heaven a rose is on the table
Which you look at instead of writing your poems or your prose
You look at the bug asleep in the heart of the rose

You recognize yourself in the mosaics of St. Vitus
You almost died of grief that day
You were Lazarus crazed by daylight
In the Jewish quarter the hands on the clocks go backward
And you creep forward through the story of your life
Climbing to the Hradchin in the evening and listening
To the Czech songs in the cafés

Here you are in Marseilles amid the watermelons

Here at Koblenz at the Hotel of the Giant

Here in Rome sitting under a Japanese medlar tree

Here you are in Amsterdam with a woman who you think is beautiful
      but is really ugly
She will wed a student from Leyden
You can rent rooms by the hour *Cubicula locanda*
I remember the three days I spent there and the three at Gouda

You are in Paris summoned before a judge
Arrested like a common criminal

You journeyed in joy and despair
Before you encountered lies and old age
Love made you suffer at twenty at thirty
I've lived like a fool and wasted my time
You no longer dare to look at your hands and now I feel like crying
Over you over the one I love over everything that has scared you

Eyes full of tears you look at the immigrant families
They believe in God they pray the women nurse their babies
They fill the Gare St. Lazare with their smell
Their faith in the stars rivals that of the three magi
They're hoping to gain some *argent* in the Argentine
And return to the old country with a fortune
One family takes a red eiderdown with it as you take your heart
      wherever you go
This eiderdown and our dreams are equally unreal
Some refugees stay in furnished rooms
In the rue des Rosiers or the rue des Ecouffes in the slums
I have seen them at night walking
Like pieces on a chessboard they rarely move
Especially the Jews whose wives wear wigs
And sit quietly in the back of the shop

You stand at the counter of a seedy café
A cup of coffee for a couple of *sous* with the other outcasts

At night you go to a famous restaurant
These women aren't cruel they're just wretched
Each even the ugliest has made her lover suffer

She is the daughter of a policeman from Jersey

I hadn't noticed the calluses on her hand

I feel sorry for her and the scars on her belly

I humble my mouth to the poor girl with the horrid laugh

You're alone day breaks
The milkmen clink their bottles

The night slinks away like a half-breed beauty
Ferdine the false Leah on the lookout

The brandy you sip burns like your life
Your life that you drink like an *eau de vie*

You are walking toward Auteuil you intend to walk the whole way
        home
To sleep with your fetishes from Oceania and Guinea
There are Christs in different forms and other systems of belief
But Christs all the same though lesser though obscure

Farewell farewell

Let the sun beheaded be

In Paris in the 1970s I came across *je-m'en-foutisme*, an attitude toward life predicated on the last thing that Rhett Butler says in *Gone with the Wind*. The indifference expressed in Apollinaire's "Hôtel" is in line with (or in anticipation of) this attitude.

Hotel

—a translation of the poem by Guillaume Apollinaire

My room's the shape of a cage
The sun crooks his arm through the bars
But I, who smoke to make mirages,
Let the flame of day light my cigarette
I don't want to work I want to smoke

I was struck, when I read *A Room of One's Own*, by how many sentences begin with "But"—how Virginia Woolf's prose pivots on this elastic conjunction.

Poem in the Manner of Virginia Woolf

But I can hear your protests. But we thought you were going to tell us how to live. But in order to make amends I shall offer you an opinion. But it is as a woman I speak. But what is interesting about the sexes is how few of them there are. But what is important is not what we have in common but what distinguishes us. But a woman needs five hundred a year and a room of her own however small. But memory enlarges it however small. But why are women poor? But are they as incapable of education as Napoleon thought? But men as mean as Mussolini despise them.

But I had escaped the poison of fear and bitterness. But my heart had leapt. But I sketched the ugly important professor writing his great book upon the mental, moral, and physical inferiority of women. But what is amusing now was once desperate earnest. But it is very well for you to scoff, you who have rooms of your own and five hundred a year. But Keats but Tennyson but the men or women of genius. But one can take an apple and say Newton was the genius who discovered the laws of gravity and Newton was a woman. But to return. But how will this richly detailed tapestry be affected by the sex of the novelist?

But how impossible it must have been. But the values of women differ from those of the other sex. But these difficult questions lie in the twilight of the future. But alas I died. But alas I did what I was determined not to do. But the blame rests no more upon one sex than upon the other. But I read on.

But if you write what you wish, that is all that matters. But a shadow shaped something like the letter "I" got in the way. But I turned a page or two. But . . . I had said "but" too often. But it is fatal for anyone who writes to think of their sex. But I maintain that to work, even in poverty and obscurity, is worthwhile.

An art critic from Australia asked me if there is a Kafka Street in New York City. Yes, I answered, "but you can't tell where it is."

On Kafka's Birthday

Franz Kafka was born today. In the black-and-white Prague of his boyhood, the sun shone yellow on the gray pavement. Debates were held in the cathedral on Sundays. The rituals of life were celebrated with frankincense and myrrh. Every man had the right to a trial. Behind the mound above the hill on the outskirts of the medieval town stood a castle. Rumors of its existence encircled the turrets of the structure like swarms of hornets. Kafka listened.

Franz Kafka was born on July 3, 1883. When he began to compose the stories on which his enduring fame is based, he chose to write in German. He knew that he was born on the day before the day the United States was born. This, he joked to Jaspers on one of their walks, is what prompted him to write *Amerika*.

Franz had a father. His father had a store. It was always three o'clock. The father's example made the son loathe himself. The castle existed in his mind like a bird on a branch, singing in the darkness.

Hermann and Julie Kafka did what they could. He was their firstborn. He arrived a year after they were married. Two other sons died as infants. What was the effect on young Kafka? "Difficult to say," Professor Sonnenschein said. Three younger sisters survived. The brood was brought up by governesses.

Kafka was named after Franz-Joseph, the old monocled emperor of the German-speaking Austro-Hungarian Empire that spanned the ancient capitals of Prague and Vienna and Budapest. The drama of

Kafka's life was the crumbling of that empire. He took a job in 1907 with the Assicurizioni Generali Insurance Company. The hours were long, the work mind-numbing, the offices filthy, the girls unhappy, the boys guilt-ridden, the hypocrisy contemptible. Then, in 1908, he found the ideal line of work for a man of his extraordinary imagination. He got a job with the Workers' Accident Insurance Institute. An executive in the human resources department of a major university advises me that Kafka's practical expertise in workers' compensation issues of his own era would have equipped him to deal with our own. "Better than having two master's degrees," she said.

But there wasn't enough time. There wasn't even time enough in a lifetime to travel from one little Russian village to the next. "Where are you going?" they asked. "Away from here," he would say. But every time he reached the train station, the man at the ticket booth wore a policeman's badge. He chuckled benignly and told him to go home: "Give it up." It was exactly three o'clock. The world made perfect sense. The state was an impartial executioner, killing the guilty and the innocent alike. But if words were spears, he had his store of weapons, too, and if there were time he would compose a petition impossible to refuse.

Kafka did not want to become famous. "Posthumous fame is not the best kind," he said. "It is the only kind."

In his diary Kafka wrote that coitus is "the punishment for being happy together."

(July 3, 2010)

Limiting myself to three words per line, I sought the jagged edges of a William Carlos Williams poem. I put in plums, his favorite fruit, and aimed to capture something lascivious in Williams's genial imagination by way of the story of Susanna and the Elders, as Williams treated Brueghel's paintings in such poems as "Hunters in the Snow" and "Landscape with the Fall of Icarus."

Poem in the Manner of William Carlos Williams

As the rain
washes her hair
the plums red

in the bowl
on the table
with their dark

red rind wait
for her eyes
to see them

her hair still
wet still full
of suds as

three old men
watch her touch
she sees them

look at her
in the painting
of Susanna bathing

Sometimes a poem can have it both ways—it can be an utterly sincere complaint about an academic institution and it can undermine the complaint merely by adopting the accents of a discredited speaker.

Poem in the Manner of Ezra Pound

If Ezra Pound were alive today
　　　　(and he is)
he'd be teaching
at a small college in the Pacific Northwest
and attending the annual convention
of writing instructors in St. Louis
and railing against tenure,
saying tenure
is a ladder whose rungs slip out
from under the scholar as he climbs
upwards to empty heaven
by the angels abandoned
for tenure killeth the spirit
(with tenure no man becomes master)
Texts are unwritten with tenure,
under the microscope, *sous rature*
it turneth the scholar into a drone
decayeth the pipe in his jacket's breast pocket.
Hamlet was not written with tenure,
nor were written Schubert's lieder
nor Manet's *Olympia* painted with tenure.

No man of genius rises by tenure
Nor woman (I see you smile).
Picasso came not by tenure
nor Charlie Parker;
Came not by tenure Wallace Stevens
Not by tenure Marcel Proust
Nor Turner by tenure
With tenure hath only the mediocre
a sinecure unto death. Unto death, I say!
WITH TENURE
Nature is constipated the sap doesn't flow
With tenure the classroom is empty
                    et in academia ego
the ketchup is stuck inside the bottle
the letter goes unanswered the bell doesn't ring

You can get a lot out of a Millay sonnet even if all you get to see are the opening and closing words of the lines.

Two Poems in the Manner of Edna St. Vincent Millay

1.

I, presently,
And jest;
And see,
And breast;
And all my pretty follies flung aside
That gaze,
Naked pride,
Spread ways.
I remained
But one more dream,
Cherish gained,
And supreme,
A ghost you knew
Who would have loved you in a day or two.

2.

What and why,
I have forgotten, and what arms have lain
Under head: but rain
Is full of ghosts that tap and sigh
Upon reply,
And pain
For unremembered lads that not again
Will cry.
Thus the lonely tree,
Nor one,
Yet before:
I have come and gone,
I, me,
A little while, no more.

Judging from the efforts of Hart Crane and Vladimir Mayakovsky, the Brooklyn Bridge may be the single most inspiring architectural structure in America. I made this translation in 1999 when I was asked to read a poem about a bridge at a public event and no existing translation conveyed anything more than a hint of Mayakovsy's grandeur and irony.

Brooklyn Bridge

—a translation of the poem by Vladimir Mayakovsky

Hey, Coolidge,

           shout for joy!

I've got to hand

           it to you—

with compliments

           that will make you blush

                      like my country's flag

no matter how United

           States of America

you may be!

As a madman

enters a church

or retreats

to a monastery,

pure and austere,

so I,

in the haze

of evening

humbly approach

the Brooklyn Bridge.

Like a conqueror

with cannons

tall as giraffes

entering a besieged

city, so, drunk

with glory,

higher than a kite,

I cross

the Brooklyn Bridge.

Like a painter

      whose smitten eyes pierce

            a museum Madonna

through the glass of a frame,

          so I look at New York

               through the Brooklyn Bridge

and see the sky and the stars.

New York,

      hot and humid

          until night,

has now forgotten

       the daily fight,

          and only the souls

of houses rise

     in the serene

        sheen of windows.

Here the hum

of the El

can hardly be heard,

and only by this hum,

soft but stubborn,

can you sense the trains

crawling

with a rattle

as when dishes clatter

in a cupboard.

And when from below,

a merchant transports sugar

from the factory bins,

the masts

passing under the bridge

are no bigger than pins.

I'm proud of just this

mile of steel.

My living visions here

stand tall:

a fight for structure over style,

                the calculus of beams of steel.

If the end of the world should come,

                    wiping out the earth,

                        and all that remains

is this bridge,

          then, as little bones, fine as needles,

                        are assembled into dinosaurs

in museums,

        so from this bridge

                the geologists of the future

will reconstruct

        our present age.

              They will say:

This paw of steel

          linked seas and prairies.

                    From here,

Europe rushed to the West, scattering

                Indian feathers

                                                    to the wind.

This rib

          reminds us of a machine—

                    imagine having the strength,

while standing

          with one steel leg

                    in Manhattan,

to pull Brooklyn

          toward you

                    by the lip!

By these cables and wires

                    I know we have retired

                              the age of coal and steam.

Here people screamed

          on the radio,

                    or flew in planes.

For some life was a picnic;

                    for others a prolonged

                              and hungry howl.

From here desperate men

        jumped to their deaths

                in the river.

And finally I see—

        Here stood Mayakovsky,

                composing verse, syllable by syllable.

I look at you

        as an Eskimo admires a train.

I stick to you

        as a tick to an ear.

Brooklyn Bridge,

        you're really something, aren't you?

When I read Mayakovsky's "Cloud in Trousers" aloud to my friend the composer Lewis Saul, he borrowed the construction and playfully labeled me a "giant in slippers."

Poem in the Manner of Vladimir Mayakovsky

Like a giant in slippers reading
the morning news of an event that
hasn't yet happened I wear my robe
of authority like the majestic girth
of a great detective my job
to puzzle out how we got to this
stalemate with its tragic
inevitability can I retrace
the moves the sacrifice of a pawn
to support the bishop's attack?
My backbone is my flute:
you play it, I sing, it hurts.
The words fly from my mouth
like people jumping off a bridge
in flames and in the city of my heart
that bridge is a temple
and I am a boy who sings in the choir
of the temple that is burning
so I cannot sing O Mother forgive me

Dorothy Parker blended craft with acid wit in her aphorisms ("Brevity is the soul of lingerie") and light verse.

Poem in the Manner of Dorothy Parker

Dorothy Parker
who wrote witty stories,
did not foresee
that spectacles would be-
come fashion accessories.
"Men seldom make passes
At girls who wear glasses."

And today,
in Washington Square Park
I thought of her, Miss Parker,
and what she might say
assessing the spectacles of our day:
"Even the nicest lasses
Have tattoos on their asses."

In her poems, Marianne Moore incorporates quotations to advance or complicate an argument. It is as if her mind in action were a vast collage of sources from the scholarly to the populist.

Poem in the Manner of Marianne Moore

If "diligence is to magic as progress is to flight"
then it is the mere "semblance of speed" that "attaches
to the scarecrows of aesthetic procedure." As in the case
of elephants and magic carpets, what wins may be called
"prosaic necessities," not to be confused with "curios."
But if diligence is to effort as victory is to endurance,
then the elephant out-tortoises the hare
because speed is to value as the cosmetic industry is to beauty.
There is, besides, a difference between the semblance of speed
and its substance, and the intention counts as the deed
only in the minds of "the unfulfilled men who till the fields
and the women who wait for them at dusk"
in the plantation there never was in the antebellum South.
The women knew where they needed to go, but chance "played its
         art,"
and the results were what they were because
a "tough-grained animal" puts to shame the aesthetic procedures
of public statuary in the far reaches of the baseball stadium,
and because, as the Yankee catcher told his adoring fans,
"If you don't know where you're going, you might not get there."

As a native New Yorker I seem to be especially receptive to the view of the city as it presents itself to foreign eyes—those of Lorca, for example, in *A Poet in New York*.

Poem Ending in a Phrase
by Federico García Lorca

The last time I saw Lorenzo
he was wearing a blind man's dark glasses
and holding the leash of a seeing-eye dog

though he isn't blind
and he doesn't have a dog
and his name isn't Lorenzo but Bruce.

Who can explain why a man might dance
on the ledge outside his office
five flights above the Hudson River?

The city with five boroughs and two thousand bridges
fits on one side of the coin
my father gave me to give to a beggar.

It is gone from my pocket as I look out the window
on the day of my old friend's funeral,
and the stock exchange becomes a pyramid of dawns.

O my great river, treat me as you would a sailor!
I hear Harlem murmur through elevator shafts.
This is not hell. This is a fruit stand.

No one sleeps. Everyone dreams. And you, Walt Whitman,
bearded with butterflies, are eyed by virile comrades
pointing you out in bars: "He's one, too."

At Cambridge University I chose modern French literature as one of my fields of specialization. This justified my frequent trips to Paris. Henri Michaux's sometimes combative prose poems, which I read in the cafés of Montparnasse in 1972, came as a liberation to one who had been governed by the spirit of Wordsworth's "Ode to Duty."

Poem in the Manner of Henri Michaux

My enemies used to annoy the hell out of me with their fake cheerfulness, their pathetic need to be liked, or their drive to dominate every conversation. And I would stand there and let them do it to me. That was my way of being, and I couldn't change it any more than a boy can recover his innocence after the invention of sex. Nature was a goddess, and I was her slave. That was how I reasoned. But in those days I was reading Rousseau, who put the craziest notions in my head, and I memorized them, bowing to my fate as to an audience clapping its hands after the play.

No more Rousseau. From now on I will recite sonnets to girls seen in the street, and on the subway I will recognize the signs of desire in her eyes still sleepy with last night's dream, and in the evening I shall lift a glass and arrange for the ex-partners to embrace after years of bickering: they shall be happy, and I shall cross the little bridge east into the Bronx on 207th Street or the one going north on 215th Street and I will visit her at night, every night. Greater than opium or German philosophy to Coleridge will the scent of her being be to me.

One of Hemingway's secrets is that he, who sometimes affects to hold the poetic in contempt, wrote narrative prose that comes closer to exemplifying a species of poetry than any of his contemporaries.

Poem in the Manner of Ernest Hemingway

The little Italian major had a bad stutter. It was impossible to take him seriously. "You," he said, "have given more than your life." Well, it was a rotten way to be wounded, but Italy in the war had been swell, and the hospital in Milan where it rained that fall was swell, and Paris was swell when he lived there with his wife and they had been happy in the winter. Later there was the case of the Spanish waiter in the café in Madrid. At two he drank one last brandy and walked home muttering the Lord's Prayer in Spanish. Why can't you sleep? Because I have insomnia, the man said with simple dignity. I say, old pal, let's utilize this pouch full of wine that was cheap but good. So we utilized the wine and then I utilized the American girl who looked bright and said meaningless things over her second stinger at the café near the station. She had gotten herself knocked-up again. By whom this time? He didn't want to know. He had insomnia. That was why he couldn't sleep. He would utilize the time by writing stories. They would be simple and they would be true and there would be girls in cafés saying witty meaningless things and they would drink stingers and have a swell time. That was what you told yourself in the hospital in Milan.

The epigraph inspired this homage to the blind librarian and fabulist from Argentina.

Poem in the Manner of Jorge Luis Borges

The Braille flowers of remote perfume.
　　　　—Juan Manuel Roca

In the library of the blind I know
there is another man with my name
but without my memories.
I move my queen's pawn.
The flowers outside are so aromatic
the odor is stronger than the dust
of books, longer-lived than the lust
of old men. Your rooks attack.

Yet I know there is another who
cannot sleep in the country of false
resemblances where there are no
libraries for the blind, no mazes
in which the implacable agent
of His Majesty's government
confronts the spy with whom he may
discuss Borges before he shoots him.

Part Four

The industrious Neruda wrote odes to many things—including laziness.

Poem in the Manner of Pablo Neruda

Yesterday I was too lazy to write this poem.
So I wrote an ode to laziness
and put in yellow birds and purple plums.
I closed my eyes and wrote an ode to sleep.
I opened them and conceived of odes
to streets, rain, wine, a beautiful nude,
my clothes waiting for me to wear them,
my toolbox, my medicine chest—
but these I left unwritten.
Laziness demanded it. She was a beautiful nude,
and we sat on the porch and watched the storm.
And I didn't write an ode to the storm and an ode
to dying in Paris on a Thursday afternoon,
an ode to dusk on a lonely country road,
an ode to chaos (the sea) and an ode to form,
to books, to Buddhism, to the stars and moon.

Tennyson in "In Memoriam" is the acknowledged master of the ABBA stanza form, but as practiced by Auden it has a particular appeal—it's like a rhyme sandwich, one rhyme incorporating the other.

Poem in the Manner of W. H. Auden

Don't bet on a team on a losing streak,
Don't get ahead at others' expense,
In affairs of the heart don't sit on the fence,
Forget your dream of learning Greek.

The body bleeds; the soul stays young.
In public squares stand statues of chefs.
The partisan crowd heckles the refs.
Boy meets girl, inserts his tongue.

When her body became the landscape,
The factions, warring for control
Of the passes and the border patrol,
Could tell that the hills had changed shape.

O as I took a walk in the rain,
I missed the moon, I wanted you,
There was myrtle and there was rue,
As I walked with you in the rain.

The young Auden wrote high-spirited songs that retain their buoyancy even when the subject matter is dire.

Due Diligence

—after W. H. Auden

They didn't do their due diligence.
They didn't do it,
And now they rue it,
And how they will rue not doing it
With vigilance, when they had the chance.
They talked the talk but didn't dance the dance.

They committed the folly
Of failing to follow the lolly.
They didn't learn about the booze,
They didn't learn about the flooze,
The smack, the jack, and the lolly.
And, in short, they missed the trolley.

They overlooked some obvious flaws.
Why? Was it arrogance
Or the need to spare the expense
Or just a lack of common sense?
Who can say? Whatever the cause,
They failed to observe the clause.

They didn't do their due diligence.
They didn't do it,
And now they rue it,
And how they will rue not doing it,
How they will rue the day
They didn't do their due diligence.

Eric Ambler inherited the basics of the spy story from Somerset Maugham and proceeded to bring the genre to its romantic fulfillment in a handful of prewar novels, such as *Journey into Fear* and *A Coffin for Dimitrios*. In my twenties, I traveled often between London and Paris and found Ambler's novels ideal reading for the journey.

Poem in the Manner of
an Eric Ambler Spy Novel

The man opposite him in the railway compartment looked familiar, and the Belgrade police chief with the lisp and the condescending manner had warned him to trust no one. Someone had tried to shoot him last night. It was a ridiculous mistake. He was no spy. He was a civil engineer: an ordinary Englishman, stoic, laconic, with a nose for good wines and a passion for jazz. He had come to Milan on holiday with his wife, and had stayed on a few extra days when she returned to London and her newspaper job. He had enjoyed his solitary walks and museum visitations, had savored his evening aperitif and postprandial brandy, until the bullets in his hotel room made the safety he had taken for granted seem a flimsy illusion. How could he have been so naive? There were killers out there, men who killed for no reason, out of rage, or for cash, or for some fanatical cause based on ancient hatred, medieval doctrine, or charismatic dictator. You couldn't get away from the danger, it was all around you like the germs of a new disease. It made every thoroughfare a dark frontier that you had to cross whatever the consequences. You couldn't avoid it. You were involved from the moment you agreed to talk to Frau Zimmer about her late husband in Geneva. What could you have been thinking? The fat man with the cigars in Zurich, the Spaniard with the scar, the flirtatious Italian woman with the high cheekbones at the bar—any of them could be the killer.

At dinner he felt he got the better of Crandall, his conversational nemesis in these group affairs, but even Crandall's cheap date could tell he was rattled. He should have gone straight to the British Embassy. It was too late now. If his dreams were a dress rehearsal for the waking nightmare of the day, a test run for an ordeal requiring all the physical courage he could muster, he knew he was in for it. He thought of his wife in London but couldn't call her image to mind as he lay in the dark unable to sleep, feeling guilty and alone, all all alone, alone on a wide wide sea . . . Yet he woke up on terra firma, in his hotel room in Villefranche, refreshed. It was much better in the morning, it was always better in the morning, with the cool sunlight moving among the cypresses and the umbrella pines. The powerful smells of coffee and tobacco greeted his nostrils in the little café on the corner where he had drunk Ricard with that brash American who knew more than he was letting on. But that was just a disagreeable memory. The air today was crisp like a premonition of April. He hadn't felt so happy to be alive in years.

Although Robert Lowell did not write villanelles, I felt that a form approaching the requirements of the villanelle, with its insistent repetition, was the right choice. The poem repeats a fragment of Lowell's line "Yet why not say what happened?" amid other images and phrases lifted from his work.

Poem in the Manner of Robert Lowell

I don't believe what I just saw.
My hands touched what my heart hurt not.
Yet why not say what?

Spiders in nuclear clocks break no laws.
Skunks on summer eves tie no knots.
I don't believe what I just saw.

Couples neck, my own neck's hot.
My eyes can see the work of my claw.
Yet why not say what?

Say not which nuncle torched the straw
Or why the deed betrayed the thought.
I don't believe what I just saw.

The grease is servile in the parking lot
And fatal the leering flatterer's flaw.
Yet why not say what?

Crows when scared go caw;
Saucer magnolias stick in my craw.
Yet why not say what?
I don't believe what I just saw.

The end-words of this poem spell out a line from Gwendolyn Brooks's "Negro Hero." It is an example of the method of composition that Terrance Hayes calls the golden shovel.

Poem Based on a Line from Gwendolyn Brooks

Let us stay here, you and I.
True, I was nervous—very, very nervous I had
been and am—but it remained possible to
know the change and feel it. In fact it gave me a kick
to eat their food, drink their wine, love their
women, pray to their god, obey their law,
and that is what I did. Into
my ears their
words entered and set my teeth
on edge, and in
the ensuing parade of vices, no order
went unheeded, with progress unimpeded, to
no end if not to save
me, you, him, her, us, and even them.

Charles Bukowski's artistry is concealed by a ruffian posture and a command of the vernacular that make his writing seem artless and therefore brutally convincing.

Poem in the Manner of Charles Bukowski

You do what you want,
I'll do what I want,
and we'll see which one of us
gets to the twenty-dollar window
in time for the fourth race at Del Mar.

On the goddamn radio
that's always playing
in my bitch's kitchen,
I heard some East Coast big-shot author
say he needs to jerk off before he can write.
All is I can say is fuck that shit.

I hate poets who beg you
to like them because you feel sorry for them.
Do not feel sorry for me.
I won on Bitches' Brew in the fourth
and went home and drank
a fifth of bourbon
and got laid.

As a freshman at Columbia, intoxicated by poetry, I joined *The Columbia Review*, headquarters for a clever and heady bunch of literati who had studied with Kenneth Koch and were big converts to the New York School before anyone else had heard of it. In "Permanently," one of Kenneth's best known poems, the nouns and verbs are said to create a sentence while an adjective "walked by, with her dark beauty."

Ode on Punctuation

A poem without punctuation is female.
        —Pauline Ambrozy

The comma is female,
The exclamation point male,
The semicolon is fem bi-curious sub 29 Virginia.

The apostrophe is prosperous, possessive (femme)
The colon looks both ways before crossing the street (m).
The fast-running dash can't make up his mind
about the curvaceous question mark lurking in the lobby. What to do?
The parenthesis (f, 30) needs attention and keeps interrupting.

Thus the sentence moves
from the solace of day
to the lunacy of night
in a dependent clause beginning "although."

111

Although it is past curfew,
the nouns in the woods
conjugate the verbs
unattended by adjectives and adverbs.

And the sentence drives to a climax
and ends in a classic final male full stop.

I like emulating Frank O'Hara, who regarded Rachmaninoff's birthday as a fit occasion for a poem.

On Marilyn Monroe's Birthday

On Marilyn Monroe's birthday I have
to catch my breath running
as a receiver catches a football,
shakes off tacklers, glides down
the sidelines to the end zone as
the game clock runs out or
like a fisherman angling for
trout, turning over phrases
until I feel a tug, catch a bite, that's
what this jolt of morning joe, like "Joltin'
Joe" DiMaggio, has done to me but if
I could calm down long enough to stop
hurrying and concentrate on the lawn
in front of me the wind at my back the laughter
from Alexander Pope's dagger-like couplets
still echoing from last night's reading
of *The Dunciad*—or maybe just to clear
the mind of words, all of them, including
the words that keep coming even now
—if I could look at the trees darkening
as a cloud covers the sun, look at the grass,
the myrtle, the pine needles, the maple leaves

and the one rhododendron the deer have not devoured,
what then? After ten minutes of bliss,
I shall return to my mind, and she will be singing,
"After You Get What You Want, You Don't Want It."

(June 1, 2013)

In college many of my friends and I wrote "I do this I do that" poems in the manner of Frank O'Hara's *Lunch Poems*. On the eighth day of the eighth month in the eighth year of the new millennium I listened to a Debussy rhapsody and contemplated the year it was written and the birth date of its composer.

08/22/08

Today in 1862
Claude Debussy was born.
I remember where I was and what I was doing
one hundred years and two months later:
elementary algebra, trombone practice,
Julius Caesar on the record player
with Brando as Antony, simple
buttonhook patterns in football,
the French subjunctive, and the use
of "quarantine" rather than "blockade"
during the Cuban Missile Crisis.
It was considered the less belligerent word.
Much was made of it in 1962,
centenary of Debussy's birth.
And if today I play his *Rhapsody*
for Saxophone and Orchestra
for the ten minutes it requires of
my undivided attention, who will attack me for
living in Paris in 1908 instead of now?

Let them. I'll take my stand,
my music stand, with the composer
of my favorite *Danse Tarantelle*.

"Every woman adores a Fascist" is Sylvia Plath's most controversial line. This poem resulted from thinking about various substitutes for "Fascist" in that formulation.

Poem in the Manner of Sylvia Plath

Every woman adores a dunce,
Every woman has done it once.
Her pantyhose get in a twist.
She went to bed with her therapist.

Meanwhile you stare back at her,
You feel her eyes on you in the mirror:
You are not cruel but cannot lie,
You who look so sadly like Adlai

If only Adlai were a jujitsu Jew.
Will he tell you what to do do do?
Your pretty heart broken in two.
Every woman adores a Republican

And loves her Daddy if she can.
Ask her after she's been kissed
Before she gets her panties in a twist.
Every woman adores a Fascist.

Reflecting her wide erudition and her boundless curiosity, Susan Sontag's journal entries read like poems or like pretexts for poems.

Poem in the Manner of Susan Sontag

The "infinity of couples": a novel in the form of a diary, dates with no entries beneath them. Is the greatest art born of ignorance?

Consider the orgasm in *L'Année dernière à Marienbad*, where, in a tryst amid emerald gardens, the man and the woman negotiate the secret passage between depression and anger.

One criticizes others for what one despises in oneself. Therefore I am playing the part of myself in this marriage. *One criticizes oneself.* Criticism is the intellect's revenge on art. *One criticizes history, which means the world.* I am a recluse or a delinquent—in other words, a writer.

The worst is not the punishment but the lie. And yet I have lied. And yet I wonder about the contempt I continue to feel for others whether I wonder about it or not.

When you get to the bottom, it will be a false bottom, with a false one beneath it, and when you get to the true bottom beneath that one, you hear a knocking from below.

Decorations: the "fruit salad" (medals on the general's chest). Declarations: Pop Art (Andy Warhol's *Kiss* but not his *Empire State*

Building) is Beatles Art. Death is photography. So is pornography. If I lived within a movie it would be *Ma Nuit Chez Maud*. So much in life can be enjoyed once you get over the nausea.

Jasper says, voyeurs are usually stupid and often impotent.

"There is another world but it is this one" (Yeats).

All pain enrages. You can't write about it, you can only live it, as Kafka said about Tolstoy.

The simplicity of Joe Brainard's "I remember" formula has inspired countless imitations, many of them ingenious. None can match Brainard in charm and unaffectedly naive self-presentation, but that doesn't stop us.

I Remember

—after Joe Brainard

1.

I remember high school and wanting people to call me Dave.
I remember a truck driver named Dave.
I remember when my older sister was sixteen and she and two
    girlfriends went on a triple date with boys named Fred, Steve,
    and Dave.
I remember when I didn't want anyone to call me Dave.

2.

I remember thinking that Communists didn't exist. They were
    bogeymen, invented to scare little kids, or they did exist but far
    away, in another country, or as abstract entities to be granted
    existence for the sake of an argument or the exposition of a theory.
I remember thinking that no one took drugs or was a juvenile
    delinquent except in movies.
I remember getting up each morning and vomiting on the way to

the elevated IRT stop at Dyckman Street and Nagle Avenue. Sometimes I could time it just right and hurl into a garbage can without breaking my stride.

I remember thinking that mental illness and profound sadness were two great romantic conditions.

I remember when there were two types of people, Jews and Catholics.

I remember when there were two types of people, those who were for the war in Vietnam and those who were against it, and there could be no commerce between us.

I remember that the world was divided between Yankee fans and Dodger fans.

I remember thinking that to be an avant-garde artist you had to be rich and live in Paris, preferably near the Notre-Dame-des-Champs Métro stop.

I remember when the test of a true artist was whether he admitted that money motivated him to write.

3.

I remember the first book I ever bought. It was a book of Zen koans with an orange-colored jacket and I bought it in a musty bookstore in the Village where Ben Hecto and I walked one spring afternoon in our senior year at Stuyvesant.

I remember two of the koans to this day.

I remember liking best the koan resembling the parable of wise Solomon except that two monks rather than two mothers are laying claim to a cat rather than a baby.

Nansen, the head monk, takes out a cleaver and chops the cat in two. When Joshu hears the story, he takes off his shoes, puts them on his head, and walks out of the room, and Nansen says: "Had Joshu been there, he could have saved the cat."

I remember Nansen showed the three young monks a jug of water and challenged them to define its essence without naming it. The first monk said: It is not a puddle because I can carry it. The second monk said: Freezes in winter, thaws in spring, quenches the parched lips of summer. The third monk kicked over the jug and won the competition.

(I don't remember the prize or the purpose of the competition, but that after all is the nature of competitions.)

4.

I remember "I Remember, I Remember" by Thomas Hood, whose poems I read in the gloom of a foggy November morning in East Anglia.

I remember "I Remember You," lyrics by Johnny Mercer, music by Victor Schertzinger.

I remember *I Remember* by Joe Brainard in which every paragraph begins "I remember," and the language is simple and unaffected, artless and innocent and charming.

I remember thinking that it took real genius to recall an early embarrassment or to exhibit your own naivete.

I remember discovering that I was funny.

5.

I remember the Woolworth's on Dyckman Street where they had an automatic photo booth. You put in your quarters, took a seat, and got four snapshots.

I remember the automat. There was Bickford's and there was Horn and Hardart.

I remember P.D.Q. Bach's "Concerto for Horn and Hardart," a witty title once.

I remember a dish of custard at the automat.

I remember watermelon, ten cents a pound, at the fruit stand.

I remember when white nectarines in upstate New York were the most delicious fruit.

I remember England and going into an automatic photo booth with Jeanne, a junior at Mount Holyoke, and both of us were blond and smiling and wearing trenchcoats.

I remember hitching rides with Jeanne from Oxford to Cambridge and spending the night in a bed-and-breakfast on Queen's Road.

I remember the embarrassment of the maid when she knocked on the door and opened it and saw that we were still asleep in our twin beds.

I remember writing love poems even when I wasn't in love with anyone.

I remember thinking that love without an object was pure.

I remember hearing an explosion and thinking it was just my imagination.

I remember *A Portrait of the Artist as a Young Man.*

I remember when I was in college and had one secret I kept from even my closest friends, and twenty years later I saw Bill, a newspaper editor just as he had always wanted to be, and he asked me about the secret and I couldn't remember.

I remember that Bill and I and two other guys were going to meet at the Eiffel Tower on July 4, 1999.

I remember the smell of Gauloises and Gitanes *sans filtre.*

I remember the movie about three army buddies who meet as planned at a New York bar ten years after the war, and now none of them can stand the other two.

I remember the episode of the sitcom in which Ann Sothern and three old friends meet as planned after many years and all are fabulously successful except Ann, who is Don Porter's executive secretary, but then it turns out that the other three were just putting on airs and Ann was the only honest one and so in an important way she was the most successful of them all.

I remember that the fight had something to do with a girl.

I remember the shock of finding out that girls liked sex as much as boys did—maybe even more in some cases.

I remember buying a ring at a Woolworth's in Dublin so she and I could stay together in a cheap hotel, pretending to be married.

I remember that the worst meal I have ever eaten was at a Chinese restaurant that summer in Dublin.

I remember expecting Chinese restaurants in the British Isles to serve the same dishes as Chinese restaurants in New York, where spicy Szechuan cooking had come into style.

I remember the squawk of the gulls and the gray of the sky above the Irish Sea.

Part Five

Some poems have a mind of their own. This one began as an imitation of a Bob Dylan song from *Highway 61 Revisited* and ended someplace else entirely.

Poem in the Prophetic Manner

They're kicking butt at Yankee Stadium,
They're tearing the old palace down,
The thieves have stolen the radium,
The professor's as sad as a clown.

And the widows and orphans are crying
Because they're allergic to dust,
The magazine husband is dying,
The preacher says yes, he must.

In jail when the turnkey is sleeping,
The poet picks locks in the dark.
Not all the old willows are weeping
As the pigeons come to roost in the park.

We're just a bunch of bozos.
The barbarians are back at the gate,
Though the idols are losing to Moses,
And the grocer says it's too late.

It must be my destiny calling,
It must be the onset of fall,

The clouds and the curtains are falling,
The convicts are standing tall.

O bard in the belly of the whale,
O sinner pretending to pray,
Wherever you are you're in jail,
In jail at the end of the day.

This poem was written after a bout with Max Jacob's *Le Cornet à dés (The Dice Cup)*.

Prose Poem in the Classic French Manner

When you parted the muslin curtains, the white branches of winter trees became the arms of girls in their spring frocks in April and May. There came a night you could smell the freshness. The next day I would climb out the window and join my friend Joel on the fire escape. It was the twentieth anniversary of President Roosevelt's death. The transistor radio had changed civilization in a superficial way that may have profound long-term implications. In California there was a place called Surf City where there were rumored to be two girls for every boy. In the evening, when all that remained of our high-minded talk was a momentary pause in the flow of noise, I admired the photos of girls mounted in an album as if they were postage stamps of rare value from foreign states and colonies. The arch of a bridge across a European river made me shiver with pleasure, but I couldn't rid myself of the fear I felt among these people whose grandparents they resembled. In the eyes of the comic book artist some humans looked like pigs, some like apes, and some, the noblest, like birds of prey. In my room I had a treasure chest and a forest where I placed a bunch of flowers in the crotch of a tree. But what I liked best were the two soda bottles I kept on the windowsill, concealed between curtain and glass, which under the influence of sleep and dreams turned into the heads of puppets with whom my parents had forbidden me to play.

There is no method for writing a poem "in the manner of" a decade. You have to let your intuition take over. This poem concludes with a quotation from *The Bridge on the River Kwai*, a movie released in 1957 but set in 1943.

Poem in the Manner of the 1940s

There was a time when a man's best friend was a cigarette. It was mostly the war that did it. Everyone was eighteen years old and reading comic books except for a couple of Jewish boys who packed *Crime and Punishment* and maybe even *Ulysses* in their duffel bags. Every night was poker night. Everyone looked good in a uniform.

The first days home were a challenge. Unemployed in Ohio you smoked, knocked back a whiskey, and heard Benny Goodman carry the melody and Teddy Wilson handle the bridge in "Body and Soul." And then another unfiltered Lucky, another Jack Daniel's on the rocks. Others were not so lucky. Guys died trying to escape, guys didn't bail out when their plane caught flames, guys stood up at the wrong moment and were shot in the head or chest.

Extracting a Camel from the pack and patting my pockets vainly for a match, I look at you, and you say, "Sure," and out comes your lighter.

The women in their veiled hats smoke, too, and each time she lights up, it means something, but what?

On shore leave the lieutenant, a Stanford man, has enjoyed the life of cocktails and a fun-loving army nurse on a beach in the Pacific. When he is alone, he wonders: *Who, if I died, would give a damn? So let's get on with the bacchanal.* Summoned to headquarters he learns they are sending him back to Bataan or the jungles of Burma on a joint British-

American high-risk venture. He discards his cigarette in disgust and thinks for a moment longingly of the woman with the peekaboo bang hairstyle he left behind in San Francisco. With admirable secrecy the two of them conducted the adulterous affair that would later provide him with the plots of two best-selling espionage novels. That didn't matter now. The only thing that mattered was to carry out the commands of the amiable but intransigent British officer—to give him the chance to say "Good show, jolly good show."

The 1950s had a certain glamour and every so often a different aspect of it—abstract expressionism, Miles Davis, Gene Kelly, James Dean, Marilyn Monroe—captivates the revisionist imagination.

Poem in the Manner of the 1950s

—for Larry Goldstein

Meet Doak Walker, the last of the all-American glamour boys. Say a prayer for Gil Hodges, who went O for the World Series. There was one big secret that separated the men from the boys, and that was what a woman looked like without her clothes on. A naked girl in 1959 was not the same as a naked girl in 1939 or 1919, wasn't that true? It was indubitably true, but how would we get the girls to prove it? If one had pretty breasts the boys would say she was "stacked" or had big "knobs." Of such remarks were many Friday night conversations composed. Rosemary Clooney joined Bing Crosby singing "Brazil." Sinatra at the piano smoking a cigarette pointed out that it was great to "know your fate is / where the Empire State is." As nice as it may be to travel on the camel route to Iraq, it's a whole lot nicer to wander back. That was the consensus. The center fielder with the crewcut got the girl, Grace Kelly got the prince, and the heavyweight champ retired undefeated. Bill Holden blew up the bridge but died in the doing. There were no homosexuals yet one of them was a camp counselor and was ousted one night, no heroin addicts except jazz musicians, and no card-carrying Communists except nondescript men in suits carrying briefcases with film canisters in them. The British meant well, poor suckers, but Europe was an old syphilitic with yellow teeth who smelled bad. We were the land of Captain Midnight and we took a correspondence course and we bought forty-eight commemoratives for twenty-five cents on a matchbook cover and the senators were Republicans, and Washington was first in war, first in peace, and last in the American League. The old general played golf and there were bungalow colonies in the summer and drive-ins with Deborah Kerr in *The King and I* and chow mein at the Hi Ho or the Min Ju on Dyckman Street. A red Coke machine dispensed green eight-ounce glass bottles, and Archie liked Betty but liked Veronica better, and there was a jukebox and there were hamburgers and chocolate malteds, all the things that made America great.

You could tell the market was going up. All you had to do was look at women's hemlines, which were rising. Such was "the hemline theory," which dates back to 1926 but applies with a vengeance to the 1960s, when the miniskirt took flight, and the imagination of boys took the predictable next step.

Poem in the Manner of the 1960s

Naked women are the best
You meet them in corn fields and meadows
They are naked and the moon is yellow
and it is summer with a bounty of apricots and plums
and then it is autumn and you meet them in the city
You meet the naked women in cafés
at parties or bars or art openings
Sometimes they wear sunglasses
Often they are smoking a cigarette and holding a cocktail
and there is a single ice cube in that cocktail
The naked women wear their hair in beehives
They like all-purpose black dresses
They take pride in how good they smell
And even when they are wearing their sleek black dress
and clutching their chic black pocketbook
you know they are the naked women you have dreamed of
since you were fourteen years old

The biographies of modern poets can test any poet's commitment to the vocation.

On the Lives of the Modern Poets

I have studied the lives of the modern poets
and if you're intent
on becoming a modern poet
probably the best thing that can happen to you
("best" in the sense of furthering the chances
that you'll go on to write poems and get them published
and be considered a modern poet
and win prizes
and be a name fashionable people drop
a few less each year
until the slumberous neglect of your work
is what survives it as a phantom
leg survives an amputation or a hand
continues to light a cigarette
years after you give up smoking)
is for your father to shoot your mother
and then himself
when you are eleven years old
and you hear the shots and discover the bodies
and then you are homeless but get great grades
and go to Harvard with T. S. Eliot

and everybody likes you
and nobody reads you.
Yes, you, too, can be Conrad Aiken

Conrad Aiken nicknamed T. S. Eliot "tse-tse." Nabokov said an anagram for the name is "toilets"; W. H. Auden preferred "litotes."

Poem Inspired by the Mind of T. S. Eliot

Went to *The Waste Land* last night
Fiona Shaw's one-woman show
in a derelict theater
on West 42nd Street it was
the first poem of the twentieth century
in which bad sex is a metaphor
for the failure of civilization
which is searching for a place
by a placid lake where it can have
a nervous breakdown in peace and quiet
the first poem of the twentieth century
to resemble a crossword puzzle
the clues in the form of fragments
phantom quotations and the image
of Eliot in a bedroom with a monastic bed
and a single unadorned lightbulb
in the ceiling he was the straightest-
looking poet of the twentieth century
with a superb cover, a banker's
three-piece suit, but he was as crazy
as the rest of us, with rats and bones
and dry rocks rattling around his brain
and a drowned sailor's swollen eyeballs

This cento, assembled in December 1997, was one of my daily poems—I had been writing a poem a day for nearly two years at this point. The first line is from John Donne, the last from W. H. Auden.

Cento: In a Drear-Nighted December

This bed thy center is, these walls, thy sphere,
The tarnished, gaudy, wonderful old work
Of hand, of foot, of lip, of eye, of brow,
That never touch with inarticulate pang
Those dying generations—at their song.
The One remains, the many change and pass
The expiring swan, and as he sings he dies.
The earth, the stars, the light, the day, the skies,
A white-haired shadow roaming like a dream
Limitless out of the dusk, out of the cedars and pines,
Think not of them, thou hast thy music, too—
Sin and her shadow Death, and Misery,
If but some vengeful god would call to me,
Because I could not stop for Death,
Not to return. Earth's the right place for love.
My playmate, when we both were clothed alike,
Should I, after tea and cakes and ices,
Suffer my genial spirits to decay
Upon the bridal day, which is not long?
I thought that love would last forever: I was wrong.

In the late 1960s, my college roommates and I spent countless hours listening to Bob Dylan albums.

Highway 61 (Revisited)

In the name of Abe—biblical predecessor
of honest Abe, who freed the slaves,
and also Bobby's dad—I stand at your gate
with faith equal to doubt, and I say,
look out kid, no matter what you did,
and incredulity gives way to unconditional surrender.

Abe say "Where do you want this killing done?"
God say "Out on Highway 61."
God directs traffic,
and young Isaac say it's all right Ma I'm only bleeding.
And Ma say it's all right boy I'm only breathing.
And Dad unpack his heart with words like a whore.

Young Isaac ain't gonna work for Maggie's brother no more.
Ike no like the white man boss,
and when stuck inside of Mobile to even the score
he looks at the stream he needs to cross
despite schemes of grinning oilpot oligarch arschloch
who wanna be on the side that's winning.

So he climbs up to the captain's tower and does his sinning
and has read all of F. Scott Fitzgerald's books.

He no get where he got because of his looks.
He's on the pavement talking about the government,
and he knows something's happening but he don't know what it is.
A strange man, Mr. Jones. Isaac Jones that is.

In this poem, written for my book *A Fine Romance: Jewish Song-writers, American Songs*, each line yokes together two songs—as line one yokes together lyrics by Lorenz Hart and Irving Berlin.

Poem in the Manner of a Jazz Standard

I've got five dollars and my love to keep me warm
I've got the world on a string and you under my skin
You're the cream in my coffee and driving me crazy
You couldn't be cuter and go to my head

Love is here to stay and just around the corner
Where or when I take my sugar to tea
All I do is dream of you, all of you,
You took advantage of all of me

Don't blame me or worry 'bout me
It had to be you and might as well be spring
Let's get away from it all, fall in love, face the music
And dance with me, let's do it

I got rhythm and the right to sing the blues
She didn't say yes she's funny that way
I believe in you were never lovelier
My melancholy baby my shining hour

It is expensive to quote more than three lines of a popular song, so, in writing my book on the songwriters, I attempted a kind of approximation of certain songs, such as "Accentuate the Positive."

Poem in the Manner of a Hit Song by Harold Arlen and Johnny Mercer, c. 1945

You've got to titillate
the body contemplate
the mind and wait
   for the spirit to follow.

You've got to violate
the norms liquidate
the germs and mate
   each girl and her fellow.

Don't hesitate to state
your case, because it's sweet
to be swept off your feet,
   by the handsome stud hero.

It's time to reiterate
the need to celebrate
and not be celibate
   so you don't die solo.

Acknowledgments

Great thanks to friends who read this manuscript in various stages of its progress: Amy Gerstler, Glen Hartley, Stacey Harwood, Ron Horning. It was a pleasure to work with my editor at Scribner, Ashley Gilliam. When I compare the finished manuscript with the one I originally submitted, I can see how large my debt to her is.

Poems from this book have appeared in *The American Poetry Review, The American Scholar, The Antioch Review, The Atlantic, Boston Review, Boulevard, The Common, Court Green, Cue, Green Mountains Review, Hanging Loose, Harvard Review, The Kenyon Review, Michigan Quarterly Review, MiPOesias, Mississippi Review, The New Republic, The New Yorker, The New York Quarterly, The New York Review of Books, Painted Bride Quarterly, Ploughshares, Plume, Poem a Day, San Diego Reader, Sentence, Slate, Stay Thirsty, 32 Poems, The Times Literary Supplement, Valley Voices, The Village Voice, Virginia Quarterly Review.*

Two poems appeared in my book *A Fine Romance: Jewish Songwriters, American Songs* (Schocken, 2009), two in *The Daily Mirror: A Journal in Poetry* (Scribner, 2000), three in *When a Woman Loves a Man* (Scribner, 2005), and two in *Operation Memory* (Princeton University Press, 1990).